Untold Stories

UNTOLD STORIES

Protestants in the Republic of Ireland
1922–2002

Edited by
Colin Murphy and Lynne Adair

Introduction by Professor Stephen Mennell

The Liffey Press

Published by
The Liffey Press
Ashbrook House
10 Main Street, Raheny
Dublin 5, Ireland
www.theliffeypress.com

A catalogue record of this book is
available from the British Library.

ISBN 1-904148-14-X

The extract on pages 177–179 from *Rathcormick: A Childhood Recalled* by
Homan Potterton is reproduced with the kind permission of the author
and of New Island Books. © Homan Potterton, 2001

Printed in the Republic of Ireland by Colour Books Ltd.

Contents

About the Editors

Colin Murphy is a community and peace activist. He has been a member of the BBC Northern Ireland Advisory Committee and was chair of Glencree Centre for Reconciliation from 1988 to 1995. Colin retired from a business career in 1999. He lives in County Wicklow.

Lynne Adair is a co-ordinator of a life skills programme for early school leavers. She has been involved as a consultant with the Glencree Centre for Reconciliation since 1998. Lynne lives with her daughter Sorcha in Killiney, County Dublin.

Colin and Lynne operate a consultancy that offers capacity building services, especially in the sustainable development and peacemaking fields.

Preface

In an article in *The Irish Times* in July 2001, Patsy McGarry wrote that the:

> . . . "armed struggle" led to the violent creation on this island of a Catholic State for a Catholic people and a Protestant State for a Protestant people wherein the twain rarely met through a turbulent and frequently bloody 20th century.
>
> In the south after 1922, a triumphant Catholic Church showed no concern for the rights/beliefs of Protestant (or other) citizens when insisting that Catholic teaching on contraception, divorce and abortion be incorporated into the law of the new State.

We researched and edited this book at a time of huge and unstoppable changes in the makeup of this nation. Ireland today would be nearly unrecognisable to our predecessors. Momentous and wide-ranging developments are happening throughout our society, in all aspects of civic, public and private life. Ireland is no longer the land of single identity, single race, book-ended by the Roman Catholic and Protestant religions. Times are changing, the Irish face is changing and with it is changing Irish religion and culture. Ireland has entered an era where the minority religion has diversified to include many other Churches, communities, and people, neither "Roman Catholic" nor "Protestant".

And so, perhaps it was appropriate and timely to bring together collectively the voices and stories of the longstanding minority of Irish citizens — those of a Protestant faith.

When we first had the idea for this book, we were convinced that there were stories by and about Protestants in the Republic of Ireland that would surprise, delight, challenge, entertain and shock. This collection, we believe, proves the point. As Protestants ourselves, and incomers from "the North", we have experienced the positives and negatives of being in the minority in "the south". "This is your room. Breakfast is eight to nine and Mass is eleven," advises the helpful landlady in the western B&B. "So you're a Prod from the North. Thank God, for we need some honesty in this place."

We knew that anyone looking for trouble, for controversy, for a chance to "have a go" at the Catholic establishment would have an easy time. The Fethard-on-Sea boycott, President Mary McAleese (a Catholic) receiving communion in St Patrick's (Anglican) Cathedral and being criticised for taking part in "a sham", the struggle to keep pluralist medical ethics alive in the new hospital in Tallaght . . . these are all cases in point. But we wanted to go deeper, to find out what people really experienced and we suspected (rightly as it turned out) that a large number of positive stories would surface. One of our own prejudices, however, was seriously questioned. We assumed that most Protestants in the south would claim a residual allegiance to Britain. Many of the stories here challenge that assumption.

Harold Clarke describes a "happy and fulfilled childhood" and comments that "it must be admitted that to be a Protestant in the south in the middle of the last century was in most cases to be privileged to a greater or lesser extent".

But privilege was not always the lot of Protestants. Edith Newman Devlin describes her childhood thus:

> There were many poor Protestants in our school, some with no shoes, even in winter . . . lips were blue with cold and trousers as likely to be attached with a rusty nail as with a button.

Our own experience at the Glencree Centre for Reconciliation and elsewhere gives us a further perspective. In a report that we researched,[*] a wider view emerges. An examination into the state of peace building in the Republic of Ireland reveals that there is a degree of exclusion of and lack of tolerance for people of the Protestant/unionist tradition and the consequent development of two opposing, self-exclusive traditions.

> [There is a] willingness by many to allow the Irish unitary State construct to go unchallenged in spite of its manifest imperfections. [There has been a] fostering of selective cultural and historic amnesia. This distortion has many manifestations, e.g. allowing whole swathes of people to be "airbrushed" out of history if their "faces didn't fit". (Irish people who fought on the British side in the world wars of the last century; the mistaken belief that only Catholic people suffered in the famines of the 19th century . . .).

This rather bleak picture is emphasised by observations such as:

> School curricula, especially the teaching of history, were sufficiently defective to allow a student to complete an entire education cycle without really learning the history, culture and beliefs of any other tradition or religion [than that of the majority tradition].

Rigidly nationalist and majority religion mindsets have prevailed since the State's inception. A tendency exists which dodges the serious concerns of both traditions in Northern Ireland. The position of people living in the Republic, especially in the border counties and who maintain a unionist mindset, goes unacknowledged. Other obstacles that permeate Irish society are found in institutions and Churches and in the nature of civil society itself. Rigidly nationalist mindsets are found in institutions such as the hierarchy of the Roman Catholic Church, the GAA, etc., which has created a culture of adherence to unrealistic political ideals. The State's acceptance and resourcing of majority religion medical

---

[*] *Obstacles to Peace Building in the Republic of Ireland*, published by the Irish Peace and Reconciliation Platform, 2000.

ethics and denominational education have perpetuated the unjust way that non-Catholic interests and culture have been excluded.

In relation to the Constitution of Ireland, the sub-committee on Obstacles to Reconciliation in the Republic (Forum for Peace and Reconciliation) identified in 1996 that problems lay with those aspects of the Constitution "which are perceived by some not to have a fully inclusive character, such as the religious or historical references, mainly in the preamble, and the provisions relating to the Irish language, the role of women . . . [and] State aid for denominational education."

Let's get personal for a moment. A friend of ours recounts the following story. She had travelled to Belfast for an amniocentesis procedure, which at that time (1994) was prohibited in the Republic under the code of medical ethics imposed on the State system by the Roman Catholic hierarchy. On the journey home, she haemorrhaged. The nurse in the Dublin hospital where she admitted herself gave her a hard time and implied that it served her right for breaking God's law.

The stories of Protestants in the Republic are as varied and diverse as the people who tell them. There are, however, cross-cutting themes that emerge from the contributions. Prime amongst these on the dark side are the corrosive effects of the *Ne Temere* decree. Bob Abbott describes the effects of this decree, issued by the Roman Catholic hierarchy in 1907:

> The strains on mixed marriages were awful. From the wedding day, and even earlier, families and whole communities were pulled apart and even broken up in pieces in an effort to meet the rigorous Catholic demands. Then when the children came, there was more trouble, more grief and more conflict.

No good word appears from the present contributors (or from any unbiased source elsewhere that we know of) to defend this edict. Who knows the breadth and depth of the damage done to the Protestant minority in the community, not to speak of the individual parents, children and extended family members who were sundered by its tenets? How many marriages were blighted even before they were solemnised? The ministries of how many priests and ministers were challenged and compromised as they struggled to preserve a modicum of Christian love as they implemented this dehumanising and degrading process?

Meanwhile, were the Prods simply "keeping their heads down", as recounted herein more than once? The evidence is that many did just that. They went for the quiet life and coped as best as they could. As Andy Pollak says:

> I looked, usually in vain, for Protestants who had made their mark on the new State, whether in politics or public service or journalism or the arts or sport.

We were told by a person who knows about these things that Éamon de Valera was not a sectarian politician and that, if he thought about Protestants at all, he thought that they would just sort of, you know, melt away. Meanwhile, he got on with constructing the Catholic State for a Catholic people that Edward Carson was developing for Protestants in Northern Ireland. This was surely symmetrical stupidity that has delivered some of the excesses of sectarian politics that disfigure our island to the present moment.

"Different" is a word that crops up in numerous stories. Bishop Michael Mayes humorously describes witnessing a Corpus Christi procession on the streets of Dublin in the late 1950s:

> I had never before seen copes, mitres, chasubles and similar exotic ecclesiastical apparel, nor had I ever smelt the faintest whiff of incense. I stood there in gaping wonder and suddenly became aware that the multitudes had vanished. I looked around, and there they were, all on their knees, rosary beads clicking loudly, murmuring their prayers. I was the only one still standing.

The sense of separateness identified by many of the contributors was often self-imposed:

> We isolated ourselves into ghettoes in the hope of main-
> taining the Church of Ireland community. It is hard trying
> to survive as a community when we are such a tiny minor-
> ity. [Máire Roycroft]

Often, however, childhood taunts such as "proddy-woddy" went
deep, and the two communities grew into an uneasy truce in
adulthood. The casual and unexpected assumptions of the majority population can also hurt. Katherine Meyer:

> I once explained to a woman I had just met that I was an
> ordained Presbyterian minister, only to hear her introduce
> me, a few minutes later, as "Sister Katherine, who belongs
> to the Presbyterian order".

Despite the ravages of *Ne Temere,* many "mixed marriages" have
survived and prospered, often providing insights into the similarities and differences between both communities which would
otherwise be absent. Susan Walsh accurately captures how narrow this gap can sometimes be:

> Our most recent discovery is that in the nursery rhyme
> "This little piggy went to market", the Protestant third little
> piggy ate roast beef, whereas the Catholic one ate bread
> and butter.

So have times changed or are things pretty much as they used to
be? Bishop Richard Clarke observes in these pages:

> Then came the 1990s. The Church — all the Churches —
> moved from a place at the centre of Irish life to becoming,
> in the eyes of many, a pariah. Ecumenism became secon-
> dary to survival, although it should have been the opposite.
> The Churches' failures — whether the running sore of
> Drumcree or the obscene instances of child abuse — be-
> came matters for sneering and contempt to the Ireland out-
> side the pews. It was not a comfortable time to be seen as a
> Christian priest.

Occasionally still, it becomes obvious that while the (Roman Catholic) Church and the Irish State have been well and truly separated over recent decades, they are far from divorced. Fergus Ryan describes an experience in October 2001:

> In light that seemed to come from the sun of another time, ten hearses with the exhumed remains of the Volunteers executed by the British in the War of Independence crept past the great fluted Ionic columns of Francis Johnston's General Post Office in a surreal military drama suffused with subversive memories. I felt strangely confused, alienated, fearful, as if suddenly caught in a warp of years, an altered state.

The minority tradition faces many challenges in the twenty-first century. Much has changed, but much still remains to be done. There is a joint responsibility both in the Protestant community and in the wider society to promote pluralism and participation. As Archdeacon Gordon Linney reflects:

> We have come a long way . . . and there is still a long way to go, especially in Northern Ireland. Our best hope lies not in the bland uniformity favoured by some but in the inclusive diversity which is the authentic Ireland of which my community is and wants to be a part.

Archbishop John Neill similarly concludes:

> Pluralism is not to be feared. The Church of Ireland is in a position to make a serious contribution to political and social debate, reflecting diversity even within Christian perspectives — an opportunity that it has not always grasped.

These challenges and opportunities must be met with a sense of hope. The time has come for Protestantism to assert its Irishness, to participate fully in the life of the nation.

Lynne Adair
Colin Murphy
September 2002

Acknowledgements

When we were struggling to find a workable formula for this publication, we were inspired by Paddy Logue's book *Being Irish* (Oak Tree Press, 2000). We spoke to Paddy and he graciously assented to his excellent format being replicated. The Katherine Howard Foundation and St Stephen's Green Trust resourced the research element of the project. At the Liffey Press, David Givens and Brian Langan have been patient and supportive throughout. Beryl Gilmore and Margaret Murphy helped with the transcription of many of the contributions and Brendan Fogarty did likewise with photography. Professor Stephen Mennell did not stint us. He let fly with his knowledge of the subject and his Introduction is a powerful piece of work that provides an effective counterpoint to the offerings of our essayists. Finally, the contributors. Whilst many were fast off the blocks with their responses, others allowed themselves to be browbeaten and stalked until they delivered up their particular gem. We believe that their words will enlighten and inform, that their untold stories confirm that Protestants have had and will continue to have positive influences on civil society in this Republic. We thank them and commend their work to the reader. This is their book.

Dedicated to Evan Windell Jones and Sorcha Ruby Adair Dowd

In memoriam M. Aat van Rhijn (1930–2002)

Introduction

Professor Stephen Mennell

Stephen Mennell is Professor of Sociology at University College Dublin and Director of the University's Institute for the Study of Social Change. He previously lectured at the University of Exeter, England, and was Professor of Sociology and Head of the Department of Anthropology and Sociology at Monash University, Melbourne, Australia. He moved to the chair of sociology at University College Dublin in August 1993. His books include: Sociological Theory: Uses and Unities *(1974, 1980);* Norbert Elias: Civilisation and Social Process *(with Johan Goudsblom and E.L. Jones, 1989); and* The Sociology of Food: Eating, Diet and Culture *(with Anne Murcott and Anneke van Otterloo, 1992).*

Ireland is an unusual country: religion counts here in unexpected ways. In Britain, from where I come originally, or in Australia where I worked before I came to Ireland, one usually did not know and had no reason to ask about the religious background of one's friends and colleagues. If anything, it was a mark of mild eccentricity among academics if one of them proved to be a churchgoer. I personally, happily settled in Ireland for almost a decade, am a non-believer — albeit one with a great affection for the Anglican liturgy as represented by the Authorised Version of the Bible and the 1662 Prayer Book. Arriving in Ireland, I found I was constantly giving people unwitting clues to my Protestant background. I hasten to add that this never produced a hostile reaction, but it did often lead to laughter. My wife and I invited colleagues to a house warming, and I had to draw a sketch map for them to find us. Not knowing how to refer to the statue at a key point en route, I indicated it with an arrow labelled "Virgin". One young woman thought momentarily that it referred to a record store, while the rest simply burst out laughing when they received their copies. I realised I had made a mistake but was it, I asked, a British mistake or a Protestant mistake? "Oh, definitely a Protestant mistake", I was told. If I used a familiar phrase like "O thou of little faith" or "Get thee behind me, Satan", I was betraying my inheritance from King James. And then there were the usual Protestant mistakes at funerals, such as continuing the Lord's Prayer — "For thine is the power and the glory, for ever and ever, Amen" — when everyone else had already shut up. Through such little and ultimately unimportant events, I found myself more conscious of my Protestant identity than ever before. This is a minor and quite benign illustration of what sociologists call "labelling theory" — our self-conceptions are to a large extent moulded by the reactions to us on the part of other people with whom we interact. In this case, it operates with greater force simply because something like 19 out of 20 citizens of the Republic of Ireland are Catholics by background, and Mass attendance is still remarkably high by international standards; thus, Protestants seem correspondingly more distinctive.

The Republic is the only English-speaking country in which Roman Catholics constitute a majority of the population. For the majority, Catholicism came to form a most important and emotionally charged part of their sense of national identity, and Catholicism is indeed one of the traits in terms of which the Irish are perceived by the rest of the world. But the island of Ireland was politically partitioned in 1920. The majority of the population of Northern Ireland is Protestant, and for them Protestantism is an equally important part of *their* sense of identity. For about half a century, both parts of the island experienced to some degree and in somewhat different ways a lack of differentiation between

Church and State, and the concession of power to institutions that are not democratically elected nor subject to the normal forces of political reason. Lord Brookeborough, Prime Minister of Northern Ireland 1943–63, famously referred to the creation in the North of "a Protestant State for a Protestant people", and the corresponding notion of a Catholic State for a Catholic people permeated the thinking of many in the south. The enmity between North and south carried with it disadvantages — severe in the North, much less so in the south — for the religious minorities in each jurisdiction. In the North, the discrimination practised against the Catholic minority eventually led to the violent "Troubles" which have afflicted the North for the last three decades, and which may now at last be drawing to a close. The conflict has been between two communities which have used "Protestant" and "Catholic" as badges of collective identity. In the south, on the other hand, a tiny Protestant minority has lived in peace — but not entirely without its passing troubles — for many decades.

The history and politics of Ireland make it all too obvious why there is a strong emotional component to religious affiliation on this island. To understand that emotional component better, with several colleagues I have also in recent years interviewed Protestants in various parts of the Republic, and I shall draw a little on what we heard.[*]

In both jurisdictions, although much more prominently in the North, Protestants exhibit signs of a "siege mentality". In both cases, but more recently in the North, Protestants have in the past constituted a political, economic and social "establishment", yet they have become — or fear they will become — "outsiders". There are strong connections between a community's long-term fortunes and experience in the past and its "we-feelings" in the

[*] The research was conducted under the auspices of the Irish Institute for Psycho-Social Studies (IIPSS), and was financed by a grant from the Royal Irish Academy. Members of the research team were Jarlath Benson, Ken Bishop, Mitchell Elliott, Stephen Mennell, Ellen O'Malley-Dunlop, Aoife Rickard and Paul Stokes. For a fuller version of the arguments advanced in this Introduction, see the article by Stephen Mennell et al. listed under "Further Reading" below.

present. In spite of the fact that violent confrontations between Protestants and Catholics are a thing of the increasingly distant past in the south, emotional residues of the past are still present.

The Protestant community in Ireland dates from shortly after the first emergence of Protestantism in the Reformation in sixteenth-century Europe and is entangled with the ties which have bound together the history of the two islands of Ireland and Britain since the Middle Ages. Norman warriors from England had become involved in the conflicts between Irish regional magnates in the twelfth century, and the English kings had laid claim to Ireland since that time. Their claims had little practical effect beyond the limits of the Pale on the eastern seaboard. The "Old English" nobility and other English settlers in Ireland tended, so to speak, to "go native" and many of them adopted the Irish language and culture. Although English kings repeatedly strove to establish their rule in the face of many rebellions, until the Reformation religion played little part. After the Reformation, the struggle to establish an effective English suzerainty took on a religious colour. In the latter half of the sixteenth century and the early seventeenth century, Protestantism came to be identified with loyalty to the crown, Catholicism with resistance to it. Under Queen Elizabeth I of England (1558–1603) and her successor King James I of England and VI of Scotland (1603–25), "plantations" were adopted as the strategy for the final assertion of English rule in Ireland. That involved the seizure of land from the previous Gaelic or "Old English" Catholic landholders, and their replacement by English and Scottish Protestants, a seizure backed by the military power of the English–Scottish State and at least partly justified at the time in religious terms. Early plantations took place in the province of Munster, and in the Irish Midlands. The most thorough plantation, and the one with the most enduring historical consequences, however, was the plantation of Ulster. This took place after "the Flight of the Earls" in 1607, when Hugh O'Neill, Earl of Tyrone, and his allies and retinue fled to Spain. Their lands and those of their Catholic and Irish-speaking vassals were seized, and the settlers who took their place included a large proportion of Scottish

Presbyterians. Presbyterians are still the most numerous Protestant denomination in Northern Ireland, and Protestants in general still outnumber Catholics there. Further south, Anglicanism was the more common form of Protestantism, and Catholics always remained a large majority. (Although its members were a small minority of the population, the Church of Ireland was the established Church in Ireland — supported by tithes much resented by Catholics — until 1869.)

Because Irish historiography is traditionally most concerned with the manifold and indisputable injustices of *Irish* history, there is a tendency to overlook two facts: that the Wars of Religion in the rest of Europe during the sixteenth and seventeenth centuries were just as much battles for land as they were in Ireland; and that, bad as it was in Ireland, there was nothing very special about the brutality by which land was conquered and the dispossessed treated. Much the same has happened historically in most large-scale agrarian societies; to give one obvious example, the Norman conquest of England involved the dispossession of Saxon lords, and the myth of the "Norman yoke" was revived by nineteenth-century English romantic writers such as Disraeli. To recognise that Ireland is not nearly so exceptional as is often thought does not, however, help to reduce the deep-rooted resentment that is still felt.

In Britain and Ireland, the counterparts of the Thirty Years War were the civil wars of the 1640s and the subsequent invasion of Ireland by Oliver Cromwell in the 1650s. In comparison with the consequences of that terrible war in Germany, these islands escaped lightly, but Cromwell is remembered for his massacre of the inhabitants of Drogheda and other acts of ruthlessness. The outcome of the civil wars was very different in the two islands. In Britain, they eventuated — fortuitously — in two relatively evenly balanced factions within the landowning class, differing somewhat in religious beliefs and attitudes towards the powers of the monarchy. These factions formed the basis for the very gradual development of parliamentary parties and political democracy. In Ireland, the outcome was a very *un*even power ratio. The civil wars led to the formation of the Protestant Ascendancy as a ruling class whose dominance was maintained by the Penal Laws and ultimately, again, by the military power of what was now the British State. The Penal Laws were a framework of discrimination against Catholics — rigorous in principle although somewhat hit-and-miss in application — disqualifying them from holding public office and, more importantly, raising severe legal obstacles to the inheritance of land from generation to generation of Catholic land-owners. After the great rebellion of 1798, the Act of Union of 1800 abolished the Irish parliament in Dublin and thereafter the Westminster parliament legislated for Ireland as for England, Wales and Scotland. The nineteenth century was marked by agitation for Home Rule and — in the context of a large proportion of the land being owned by a minority of Protestant landlords — for land reform. Home Rule was very nearly restored on several occasions. It was resisted strongly by the Ulster Protestants and their allies in the House of Lords, and the measure was overtaken by the outbreak of the First World War. There followed the Easter Rising of 1916 and, in the wake of the execution of its leaders, the triumph of Sinn Féin in the 1918 General Election in all parts of Ireland except the north. The Sinn Féin Members of Parliament refused to take their seats at Westminster, and sat instead in the first Dáil Éireann in Dublin as the control gradually slipped from the hands of the British government. In 1920, the Westminster Parliament passed the Government of Ireland Act, which foreshadowed the partition of the island into the six and the twenty-six counties, which in turn came into effect at the end of the War of Independence. That war was concluded by a treaty, which itself became the occasion of an even bloodier Civil War between pro-treaty and anti-treaty factions within the new Irish Free State.

It is scarcely surprising that two centuries of Protestant triumphalism were succeeded by several decades of Catholic triumphalism in the south after independence, nor for that matter that partition was succeeded by a reassertion of a parallel Protestant triumphalism under the Stormont regime in the North. In the North, five decades of systematic discrimination against Catholics

— in matters of employment, housing, politics and policing — resulted in the emergence of the civil rights movement in the late 1960s, and subsequently to the low-intensity civil war involving paramilitary violence by both Catholics and Protestants (rooted mainly in working-class communities on both sides). In the south, the original Irish Free State Constitution was formally secular, and Éamon de Valera's 1937 Constitution, which succeeded it and remains in force (with amendments) today, is at least relatively non-denominational. Article 44 of the 1937 Constitution asserted the State's recognition of the Protestant and Jewish congregations in the Republic, but also "the special position of the Holy Catholic Apostolic and Roman Church as the guardian of the Faith professed by the great majority of the citizens". Article 44 was amended by referendum in 1972 to remove this phrase. The 1937 Constitution also contains other religious references. Article 6 asserts that "All powers of government . . . derive under God from the people", a phrase of apparently innocuous piety but which, the American Protestant critic Paul Blanshard pointed out in 1954 (see Further Reading below), could be interpreted as embodying the political philosophy of Pope Leo XIII and as obliquely acknowledging "the Church's supremacy over any area of democracy which the Church cared to claim as its own". Yet, unlike in the United Kingdom, where the Church of England and the (Presbyterian) Church of Scotland are each established Churches in their respective countries, there is legally no established Church in Ireland. Blanshard asserted that Ireland was a "clerical State" because of the Church's ability to influence public policy through what political scientists call "covert power", based upon a pervasive tendency for people to trim actions and policies to what they perceived and anticipated the Church would wish. But even Blanshard admitted: "Its political democracy is genuine, and it grants complete official freedom to opposition political parties and opposition religious groups."

Between formal legality and social reality, however, there was a striking gap. After independence, a very strong Catholic ethos took hold in public life, as John Whyte described in his classic *Church and State in Modern Ireland, 1923–79.* Besides the already wide-spread feeling for the majority that to be Irish was to be Catholic and that to be British was to be Protestant, arguably the promotion of a strong common religiosity helped bind up the deep divisions of the Civil War. The Catholic Church then, as now, controlled the majority of schools, hospitals and welfare services. Catholic social teaching was embodied in social legislation. Divorce, for example, was forbidden under the Constitution until a referendum in 1996; the sale of contraceptives was illegal until recent years; and abortion is still proscribed under the Constitution. Between the 1920s and the 1970s or 1980s the Catholic Church achieved what Tom Inglis has called a "moral monopoly" in the Republic of Ireland, and yet the Republic never ceased politically to be a relatively pluralist parliamentary democracy. As its monopoly has declined in recent years, the Irish Catholic Church has had to learn to behave more like just one player — albeit still a strong one — in a situation of both political and moral pluralism.

At its height, Catholic dominance found expression in a number of ways which in hindsight are probably embarrassing to the majority of Irish people today. There was extensive censorship of what now seem quite inoffensive publications. Blanshard gives a long list, in force in the early 1950s, of officially banned books; such is the distinction of the banned authors that, again in hindsight, one might consider it a humiliation for an author *not* to appear in the list. A small number of ugly incidents are also still remembered two or three generations onwards. The three best remembered are perhaps the controversies over the appointment of a librarian in County Mayo in 1931, the "Mother and Child" scandal of 1951 and the Fethard boycott of 1957.

The earliest of these three famous incidents arose from the nomination of Miss Letitia Dunbar-Harrison, a Protestant graduate of Trinity College Dublin, to the post of County Librarian in Mayo, by the Local Appointments Commission of the national government. The Commission had been established to take most local appointments out of the hands of local government, in an effort to root out jobbery and clientelism and to ensure that posts were filled entirely on professional merit. By law, the County Council was required to accept the recommendation of the Commission. But the Library Committee of the County Council, dominated by Catholic priests, refused to do so. When the full County Council refused to overturn the decision of its committee, the whole Council was suspended by the national government, and Miss Dunbar-Harrison installed in office. However, this provoked a highly effective boycott of library services in the county, and most of the branch libraries closed down. Most of the Catholic bishops argued that it was wrong for a Protestant to have such potential influence over what the Catholic majority in the county read. It became expedient for the national government to transfer Miss Dunbar-Harrison to a comparably senior post elsewhere, and the following year the incoming Fianna Fáil government under Eamon de Valera restored the County Council.

Of much greater long-term significance was the defeat of the Mother and Child Scheme by the Catholic hierarchy in 1951. The Minister of Health in the inter-party government of the day was a young (Catholic) doctor, Noel Browne. Aware that infant mortality had remained relatively high in Ireland, while in other European countries (notably in neighbouring Britain, where the National Health Service had just been established) it had fallen considerably in the course of the twentieth century, Dr Browne proposed legislation to bring in a measure of free medical care and maternal education. The Catholic hierarchy, from a mixture of motives, opposed this. The bishops were suspicious of any public provision that might impinge on its control, direct or indirect, of most of the hospitals in the Republic. But, more specifically, they were concerned that no woman should learn about contraception in the course of any programme of maternity training, and that gynaecological care should in no circumstances involve therapeutic abortion — even though Browne's scheme did not provide for either of these eventualities. On receipt of a letter from the hierarchy, the Cabinet dropped the proposal entirely, and Dr Browne resigned. The then Taoiseach, John A. Costello, stated: "I, as a Catholic, obey my Church authorities and will continue to do

so." Although a watered-down version of the scheme was subsequently enacted by the next Fianna Fáil government, and although today Ireland has very high standards of perinatal care,
this episode — by revealing very publicly that the Catholic hierarchy in those days had the power to overrule the elected government — caused grave disquiet in many quarters, and may indeed
in hindsight be seen to mark the early beginnings of the decay of
the Church's moral monopoly.

Something as private as the (temporary) breakdown of a marriage in Fethard-on-Sea in County Wexford was the occasion of
national controversy in 1957. A Catholic farmer had married a
Protestant woman in 1949, and the bride had — as required by the
Catholic Church's *Ne Temere* policy — given an undertaking that
the children of the marriage be brought up as Catholics. Early in
1957, she apparently changed her mind, and fled with her children to Belfast, from where she stipulated that she would agree to
a reunion only if her husband would agree to the children being
brought up as Protestants. In Fethard, it was rumoured that local
Protestants had assisted the wife in her flight, and in retaliation
local Catholics began a boycott of their Protestant neighbours.
Two Protestant shopkeepers lost much of their trade, a music
teacher most of her pupils, and a Catholic teacher resigned from
the local Protestant school. The Catholic hierarchy did not condemn the boycott, and one of the bishops preached of "a con-
certed campaign to entice or kidnap Catholic children and deprive
them of their faith". On the other hand, many other Catholic
voices — including that of the Taoiseach, Eamon de Valera —
were raised in protest against the boycott, which nevertheless lin-
gered until the autumn of 1957.

Times, of course, have changed a great deal since these three
still-remembered incidents, and priests are no longer able to act as
what Blanshard called "moral policemen". Inglis has traced the
decline of the moral monopoly of the Catholic Church, especially
through the impact of television and other mass media since the
1960s, and as a result of numerous clerical sex scandals in the
1990s; arguably, those scandals are as much result as cause of the

collapse of the monopoly — before, problems could just be hushed up. But the three incidents just described were, in any case, symptoms of a period of Catholic triumphalism which followed a much longer period when Protestants enjoyed a standing in Irish society out of proportion to their numbers.

To this day, in the Republic, both the minority Protestant community and the majority Catholic community are very conscious of the Protestants' former status as a powerful established group. It is not hard to uncover a historic emotional burden of guilt on the Protestant side and resentment on the Catholic. But in the meantime, the Protestants have become something of an outsider group. The process of transition from established to outsider group is only partly a matter of declining numbers, but numbers are important.

The steepest decline in the numbers of Protestants in the 26 counties occurred in the 1920s. Much of it was accounted for by the exit of the British garrison, and by the emigration to Great Britain or Northern Ireland of many who could not reconcile themselves to life in the newly independent and Catholic-dominated Irish Free State. Emigration, probably disproportionately higher among young Protestants, continued during the decades of economic and social stagnation following independence. The need to emigrate has historically been resented by people of both religions, but among Protestants the principal focus of resentment had by the 1930s or 1940s shifted to the operation of the *Ne Temere* decree. Because of its overwhelming strength in the 26 counties, the Catholic Church was able to enforce — perhaps more effectively in the Republic than in any other country — the principle that the partners to a "mixed" Catholic/Protestant marriage had to agree before the wedding that the offspring of their union would be raised as Catholics. This principle contributed to the further numerical decline of the Protestant minority, although it is difficult to compute its exact contribution. Falling numbers pose a direct obstacle to the survival of the Protestant community, because not only is endogamy difficult to sustain among such a small minority ("There are not many Protestant guys out there", as one young woman wistfully told us in an interview), but so also is the social infrastructure or networks of predominantly Protestant organisations which once existed — such as the Boys' Brigade, troops of Boy Scouts and Girl Guides, tennis clubs and so on, as well as parish congregations themselves — especially in rural areas where adherents are more sparsely scattered. Still more important for survival in country areas is ownership of land. Rural respondents in our interviews openly expressed anxieties about the attrition of "Protestant land". It was said that a large number of Protestant farmers had never married, so there were no Protestant children to whom the land could be left.

Yet it is not *just* numbers that turn an established group into an outsider group. Protestants probably never amounted to more than about nine per cent of the population in the 26 counties (Church of Ireland membership totalled 8.5 per cent in 1861). It is also — and more especially — a shift in the power ratio between groups that is the hallmark of such a transition from established to outsider status. The decline of Protestant organisational infra-structure would contribute to this shift in power, but the Protes-tant community did not become powerless. Despite the operations of the Land Commission following independence, Protestants are probably still statistically somewhat over-represented among the larger landholders. And, at least until fairly recently, there were many businesses known to be owned by Protestants and employ-ing mainly Protestants.

If their economic power persisted, however, there was a decline in the social prestige and the political power and influence the wealthier Protestants had enjoyed prior to independence. They ceased to be part of the power elite of the State. In his 1970 book, Albert Hirschman famously distinguished between *Exit, Voice and Loyalty* as three strategies available to people who feel dissatisfied with the rewards they gain from their organisational commitments. "Exit" was the choice of many Protestants in the years following Irish independence, and many of those who remained felt a loyalty somewhat divided between two States: the predominantly Catholic Free State and the predominantly Protestant United Kingdom. The least probable strategic choice would appear to have been "voice". For many years, even before independence, many Irish Protestants had felt what the Reverend John Dunlop has termed a "precarious belonging", sensing themselves as guests among what W.B. Yeats called "an unappeasable host". In consequence, those who did not exit have not been very vocal in the public domain. After some early resistance by prominent Protestants — such as Yeats, who, having become a Senator in the Irish Free State, protested that if divorce were to be made illegal, then all civil marriage might as well be abolished too — they have tended to become a silent minority. The have kept their heads down, and not rocked the boat. Victor Griffin, former Dean of St Patrick's Cathedral, Dublin, recalls how in the 1930s and 1940s his mother urged him not to make waves, "or you'll get us all burnt out". House burnings were already an unrealistic fear, but a danger then of very recent memory. More recently, some southern Protestants have said that the time has come for more outspokenness.

How important is the sense of Protestant identity today? The people in the groups we interviewed were nearly all regular churchgoers, but we asked them whether they were conscious of belonging to a wider community that included people of Protestant background who were no longer active churchgoers. The impression was that there was indeed such a wider network. One participant observed that, "Yes, of course, we all know each other", and others agreed that wherever they went in Ireland, they would know "friends of friends". Yet this sense of belonging to a wider network is two-edged: in part it reflects the very smallness of the numbers of people involved. One of the major themes to come out of our discussions was the sense of isolation felt among the Protestant community. This was perhaps particularly marked in rural areas. We heard hints at the sense of a lack of involvement in the local community produced by Protestant children going away to boarding schools. This sometimes led, at least in the past, to consequential exclusions — for example, those who had played rugby were disqualified from playing Gaelic football or hurling within the Gaelic Athletic Association (GAA). The processes of exclusion could be two-way; we heard of a family in one of the border counties who had been boycotted by their fellow-Protestant parishioners because they had sent their daughter to the local Catholic school to take advantage of its musical facilities.

Perhaps the most serious recurrently expressed grievance among our respondents was the feeling that their fellow-citizens of the Republic did not consider them to be entirely Irish, by reason of their not being Catholic. They protested that they were loyal citizens of the Republic, and descended from those Protestants who, in the 1920s, had chosen *not* to go to the United Kingdom. On the other hand, it was often admitted that for a generation or more after independence, family members had listened to British radio, read British newspapers, had pictures in their homes of the Royal Family, avidly listened to the Kings' or the Queen's Christmas broadcasts, and served in the British forces. The days have long since past when it was still possible to speak of a recognisable "ex-unionist" body of opinion in the Republic, but for the moment a lingering association of Protestantism with Britishness in the perception at least of some of their fellow citizens — or perhaps in some Protestants' *perception of the perception* of their fellow citizens — remains a problem.

Yet the participants in our study quite often understood why they should be misunderstood and even disliked by the Catholic majority. One of them explicitly asserted, and others from time to time hinted, that the severity and enmity of the Catholic Church of the 1920s, 1930s, 1940s and 1950s was "understandable", given the scorn with which Catholicism had been treated in Ireland by Protestants in previous centuries, mentioning in particular the sustained attempts to convert (or coerce) Catholics to Protestantism.

Not surprisingly, among the southern Protestants we talked to, there seemed to be considerable feelings of anxiety about the North. The militancy of Northern Protestants, as portrayed daily on television and in the press, posed a threat to the southerners' wish to believe that "we are included, things are better now". The distrust between Northerners and southerners appears to be reciprocal. The perception by some Northerners that their southern co-religionists are a silent minority, tainted by decades of accommodation and the pursuit of a quiet life, has its counterpart in southerners' view of the Northerners as intolerant and bigoted. (It should be noted that there is a very similar pattern of reciprocal perception between Northern and southern Catholics.) Southerners generally disapproved of Northern Protestants' ritual marching in an offensive way, and of their shunning of all things Catholic. The outbreak of the Troubles in 1969–70 brought these feelings very near the surface. We were told that southern Presbyterians would be much happier being affiliated to the Church of Scotland than forming a single province with Northern Presbyterians, and that the Church of Ireland had at one time come close to splitting into two separate provinces. While the view was sometimes expressed that "we'd all be better off in a united Ireland", the balance of feeling appeared to be against closer contact with the "crazy people" up there. One participant chillingly remarked that, while the Protestant minority of three per cent or so was treated tolerantly, "things would be a lot less peaceful for us if we constituted twenty per cent". (Protestants would make up about one-fifth of the total population of a united 32-county Ireland.)

Protestants in Ireland have much to be proud of, and their pride is linked to their deep wish that their religion and the Protestant community endure in the future. That future is in question, however, partly because of the sheer demographic facts posed by Catholics constituting the overwhelming majority. On the other hand, the moral monopoly of the Catholic Church is visibly weakening. Some far-seeing Protestants in our research groups hinted at a desirable eventual outcome: the "Protestantisation" of the Catholic Church itself. How likely is this to come about? Tom Inglis has argued that the Reformation is coming late to Ireland. With the decline in mass attendance on Sundays (although it is still high by international comparison), the widespread disaffection of the laity from the formal structures of the Church thanks to the recent spate of sexual scandals, and the spread of *à la carte* Catholicism (for example, in respect of contraception, abortion and divorce) — this possibility cannot be dismissed out of hand. But such a subtle ideological and behavioural Protestantisation of Irish Catholics, of course, is an outcome very different from an expansion of the Protestant community itself.

Further Reading

Blanshard, Paul (1954), *The Irish and Catholic Power*, London: Derek Verschoyle.

Bowen, Kurt (1983), *Protestants in a Catholic State: Ireland's Privileged Minority*, Dublin: McGill-Queen's University Press/Gill and Macmillan.

Dunlop, John (1995), *A Precarious Belonging: Presbyterians and the Conflict in Ireland*, Belfast: Blackstaff Press.

Griffin, Victor (1993), *Mark of Protest: An Autobiography*, Dublin: Gill & Macmillan.

Inglis, Tom (1998), *Moral Monopoly: the Rise and Fall of the Catholic Church in Ireland* (2nd ed.), Dublin: UCD Press.

Maxton, Hugh [W.J. McCormack] (1997), *Waking: An Irish Protestant Upbringing*, Belfast: Lagan Press.

Mennell, Stephen, Mitchell Elliott, Paul Stokes, Aoife Rickard and Ellen O'Malley-Dunlop (2000), "Protestants in a Catholic State — A Silent Minority in Ireland", in Tom Inglis, Zdzisław Mach and Rafał Mazanek (eds.), *Religion and Politics: East–West Contrasts from Contemporary Europe*, Dublin: University College Dublin Press, pp. 68–92.

Tovey, Hilary (1975), "Religious Group Membership and National Identity Systems amongst Adolescents in Cork", *Social Studies* 4(2), pp. 124–42.

Whyte, John H. (1980), *Church and State in Modern Ireland, 1923–79* (2nd ed.), Dublin: Gill & Macmillan.

Robert Abbott

Bob Abbott is retired from a career largely involved with marine engineering and is a voluntary Methodist local preacher of 50 years' standing. He was born and brought up in Athlone and moved to Dublin in 1944 to find a job. Bob lives in Raheny with his wife Vera, whom he married in 1953.

These days in Raheny, relations between religions, and with those who have no faith at all, are fine. Many of my neighbours are good Christians. One lady, who attends Mass every day and is a frequent pilgrim to Medjugorje, is the best collector I know for Dublin Central Mission (Methodist) and The Leprosy Mission (Anglican). When the windows in a local (north Dublin) Methodist church were broken by vandalism recently, a collection was taken up in the local Catholic Church towards the cost of repairing them.

But it was a different story in Athlone in the 1920s. Ours was an "economically challenged" family — so, for instance, there was no chance of me progressing to a Protestant secondary school. I can't recall, incidentally, that much help came our way from Protestant charitable institutions. After national school, I was lucky to find a measure of secondary education in the vocational school, which was non-denominational. The headmaster gave me a good reference so I had no difficulty in getting a job in the thriving Protestant business sector in Dublin. Later, I moved to Aer Lingus, which was completely open; nobody cared what religion you were. After that I had a series of jobs, generally in marine engineering, but I was always conscious of not having had the chance of getting a professional qualification.

Athlone was a divided and distressed town with very little in the way of opportunity for anybody, not least for the Abbotts. The town suffered economically from the departure of the British garrison and, of course, from the recessions of the 1920s and 1930s. Such Protestant businesses as there were went into decline and of course the majority were Catholic-owned and managed. In former times, the garrison officers had private incomes that contributed to the local economy but all that stopped after the garrison was stood down, just like a tap being turned off. Jobs were few and far between and, unfortunately, some powerful forces within the majority religious community saw to it that their people got whatever chances were going. More than once, my father lost jobs as a result of a priest instructing the proprietor: "You had better let him go. We don't need his sort filling scarce jobs here." Not all priests took this line but there were enough who did to make life very difficult for us. Wherever you turned, the world seemed to be against us. The Catholic boys used to call out "Proddy-woddy ring the bell, when you die you'll go to hell" when we passed by on the way to our national school. But protest or complaint was never even considered. We simply knew that we had to keep our heads down and say nothing. Nevertheless, I have never felt anything other than Irish and have no sense of being British.

In the early days of the new State, the Taoiseach, Eamon de Valera, had no sense of developing the economy, so wealth-creating opportunities, such as they were, were simply left to take their chances and wither away in the harsh, depression-ridden, protectionist climate. Such enterprises, be they British-based or Protestant-owned, that had a chance of weathering the storm were certainly not encouraged or assisted by such popular sentiments as, "Burn everything English except their coal".

Politically, however, those were interesting times. The unexpected happened on a daily basis. During the Civil War, Protestant friends in Westmeath had had a habit of keeping safe houses for de Valera's men. Such people just seemed to care for those who were on the run. It's strange to relate now that William Cosgrave, the Cumann na nGaedhael Taoiseach, always seemed to be surrendering to the priests and bishops whilst Dev's men had been excommunicated. Later on, of course, Dev had to learn to kowtow to the Church bigwigs like the best of them. Nevertheless, when Meath County Council tried to find excuses to close down a Protestant mission hall, word came from Dev's office to "leave them alone". I did note strange goings-on in an avowedly neutral country and was fascinated to see that British war planes and crews that had survived crash landings in the countryside were carefully shipped to the North whilst German equipment was impounded and their people interned.

As a child in Athlone, I remember the big May processions to the Catholic churches. Again, there was a sense of confusion. On the one hand, as children, we were scared of what we perceived to be naked triumphalism on the part of our Catholic neighbours. (In this regard, I remember wondering why eight soldiers of the Irish army were on parade, complete with fixed bayonets, marching alongside the faithful and guarding the canopied statues and the host.) On the other hand, it was the custom for the flowers for these special festivals of the Catholic Church to be provided by my family from the garden of the old Church of Ireland garrison church!

Now, of course, in 2002 the Protestant population has declined. Where did they all go? Some just melted away when the Brits left, taking their traditional businesses such as woollen mills, shoe factories, etc. Other people were intimidated out. More simply assimilated into the Catholic Church, thanks to the pressures of the *Ne Temere* decree that forced parents to raise their children as Catholics. The strains on mixed marriages were awful. From the wedding day, and even earlier, families and whole communities were pulled apart and even broken up in pieces in an effort to meet the rigorous Catholic demands. Then when the children came, there was more trouble, more grief and more conflict.

But things are better now. Ordinary people are voting with their feet. Some walk out of church forever and, thankfully, others feel free to walk into whatever church they wish.

Otherwise, a Protestant minister would not have been invited by the authorities to preside at an ecumenical carol service at the ancient monastic settlement of Clonmacnoise. Nor would I have been given the opportunity to offer the prayers for the faithful in a Roman Catholic chapel in downtown Dublin.

In conversation with Colin Murphy

Robert Ernest Armitage

Ernest Armitage was born in 1933 at Deer-park, Cloughjordan, County Tipperary, and educated at Wesley College and Trinity College, Dublin. He was Resident Master in Wesley College, teaching mainly history, geography and religious education from 1955–63 and Housemaster, Head of Geography Department and Vice-principal from 1967–93. He is the author of The Interpretation of Geographical Photographs *and* Wesley College Dublin 1845–1995, An Illustrated History. *He is a member and local preacher of the Methodist Centenary Church, Dublin.*

Roots

Our branch of the Armitage family is descended from Joseph Armytage, a wool merchant of Kirklees Priory, Brighouse, Yorkshire, where the family still resides on an estate acquired on the confiscation of the monasteries under Henry VIII (1536–39). He acquired land in County Louth in the late sixteenth century, and later moved to County Kilkenny before the family arrived in County Cork. By the eighteenth century, various branches of Armitages had arrived in Counties Tipperary, Laois and Offaly as tenant farmers. We have a family tree going back to the twelfth century due in part to the work of a Canadian cousin who obtained information from the Public Record Office in Dublin before it was destroyed in the Civil War in 1922, and in part to the records held by the Yorkshire Armitages.

My father's mother was Eleanor Mills from County Armagh who came to Cloughjordan to work in Walton's shop and who helped my grandfather build up a thriving family business along with running a farm. It was even recorded that within the extended Armitage family their marriage was opposed and she was always considered to be an "outsider".

Vision and Service

My mother was a member of the Church of Ireland but from her marriage joined my father in the tradition of John Wesley's preachers. I am most grateful for the example of their lives — loving, industrious, thrifty and sacrificing so that their seven children might have a good education. I happily attended Sunday morning and evening Methodist services, Sunday school and Saturday afternoon Junior Christian Endeavour Society meetings. My resolution at the age of about eight to be a disciple of Jesus has matured and strengthened despite the pressure of atheism and materialism. My aim is to serve my Lord. My parents' religion was no narrow piety. They were generous and friendly, as were their neighbours. My father was involved in agribusiness, requiring frequent journeys throughout the country, yet he found time to play a leading role in founding Clar Ellagh, Christian Holiday Centre, Kilkee, County Clare under the auspices of the Christian Endeavour Movement (1944) and Gurteen Agricultural College in County Tipperary under the auspices of the Methodist Church in Ireland (1946).

Community Tensions

While we were surrounded by very good Roman Catholic neighbours in Cloughjordan, I was aware of the rigid division of the community's social life into Protestant and Roman Catholic. This had arisen from the differences between the natives and the mainly Cromwellian planters who arrived in the seventeenth century. It was reflected in the ascendancy of the Anglican community in the eighteenth and nineteenth centuries and a fairly widespread feeling of Protestant superiority, the land struggles of the late nineteenth and early twentieth centuries, segregated education, the divisions of unionist and nationalist prior to 1921, the different attitudes to Sunday observance, and the dominant position of the clergy of the Roman Catholic Church post-1921. My parents feared the impact of the Church's implementation of the *Ne Temere* decree concerning mixed marriages from 1907 and felt hurt by its unfairness to the Protestant spouse in the marriage. In addition, the family had suffered threats, and the family business was robbed and unjustly boycotted in the early decades of the twentieth century. A decision was made to emigrate to Tasmania but was abandoned as an admission of defeat.

Growth in Understanding

My father earned the trust of both sides of the community and he was in time able with others to help to ease some of the tensions. He was the founding President of the Cloughjordan branch of the Young Farmers Club (1948) and later the founding Chairman of the local branch of the Irish Farmers Association (1956). Boarding school in Dublin and undergraduate studies in Trinity College, Dublin widened my horizon and enabled me to take a balanced pride in my "Anglo" and Irish cultures combined with a growing appreciation of the history and geography of my native country. Dr T.W. Moody, Professor of Modern History, Trinity College, Dublin, encouraged his students to search for the truth in the historical record, and to understand that human bias is acceptable but that prejudice is not. My parents never told their family of the horrible events of the pre-1921 Troubles and of the Civil War and so we were spared much bitterness. Yet someone has pointed out to me that if you do not know your history then you cannot learn from it.

Emigration

Five of my parents' seven children worked for short periods outside this State and then returned. All but one of their 25 grandchildren live here. My four years' teaching in a secondary school in northern Nigeria (1963–67) was an enriching experience. Coinciding with a period of inter-tribal violence, I was impressed by the students' ability to co-operate even when tribal violence reached the school campus. I gained a better understanding of the complications of the community tensions in Northern Ireland. The educational progress made by students from very humble back-grounds when given an opportunity impressed me, and I was challenged to consider the just claims of the disadvantaged no matter where they live.

The Future

Looking at Ireland today, I am concerned about social inequali-ties, greed and materialism, about the spiritual vacuum which in-creasingly exists, and the insidious effects of the abuse of drugs and alcohol on Irish society. John Wesley spoke of the Methodist people as "the friends of all and the enemies of none" and that the world was his parish. As I see it, the challenge for Protestants liv-ing in Ireland today is not so much to protest as to be good citi-zens who try to live the Gospel and who are willing to share that Christian Gospel with all who will receive it.

Bruce Arnold

Bruce Arnold is Chief Critic and Political Columnist of the Irish Independent. *Born in London in 1936, he was educated in England, at Kingham Hill School, and at Trinity College, Dublin. He is a Fellow of the College and a Doctor of Letters. He joined* The Irish Times *in 1961 and has worked as a journalist in Dublin ever since, twice winning an award for Outstanding Contribution to Journalism. He is the author of 16 books, including* A Concise History of Irish Art, The Scandal of Ulysses, *biographies of Jonathan Swift, Margaret Thatcher, Charles Haughey, Jack Yeats and Jack Lynch, as well as four novels. He has made six documentary films, including two on Joyce and two on Irish artists. He is librettist for* A Passionate Man, *an opera about Jonathan Swift.*

Faith and Identity

I was not baptised in infancy. I don't remember going to church until I was sent to boarding school at the age of seven. My first experience of religion came then. It was the winter of 1944. It was wartime, and the dormitories had to be blacked out at night with large fitted screens of black linen stretched over wooden frames. Before going to bed, we had prayers and sang a verse or two from a hymn. I remember particularly the words of Thomas Ken's wonderful hymn, "Glory to Thee, my God, this night", and the comfort I felt, the protection, of the words, "Keep me, oh keep me, King of kings, Beneath Thine own almighty wings."

Faith prospered within me and for ten years or so I enjoyed an intense and rich spiritual life. It included my baptism at the age of

14, followed by my confirmation. It also included many schoolboy debates about faith and eternity, the universe, the meaning and existence of God and one's own soul. I was a child of my time. I went to the London crusades of Billy Graham, I was captivated by the idea and then the commitment of personal salvation, and in those glorious summers of the 1950s I attended Crusader camps and London missions.

Some of this faith had rubbed off by the time I came to Trinity College in 1957. But College chapel, music, the resumed debate about the purpose of existence, restored it. Above all, both faith and religious identity played an important part in my marriage into a Church of Ireland family in Sligo. I became part of a Protestant community and have remained part of it ever since.

It was a defining experience, for me quite pivotal. It gave me identity, and I realised that identity was a significant part of Protestantism in Ireland. It had not been the same in England, at least not to my recollection. There, faith had reigned supreme. One was Christian, and the ways of expressing this were many and varied. What mattered was the faith. Identity came from elsewhere and had little or nothing to do with belonging or not belonging to a Church.

In Ireland, I learned a different order of priority. In the 1950s, when I was married, and in the 1960s when my three children were born and baptised, the community to which I belonged, both in Sligo and in Dublin, was necessarily one in which the Church of Ireland figured significantly. I was proud of the fact. It was a badge of identity. It also helped in the expression of feelings and judgements.

But it was not universally seen in that way, least of all, I suspect, in the rural community of Strandhill, outside Sligo town. There it was tribal; identifying with the Church was enough. The neighbouring farmer and his family, retired people, members of families engaged in business in the town or in the countryside there, gathered in the tiny St Ann's Church overlooking Coney Island and gave a chilly nod to the fact that they all belonged to each other.

It was a bleak sense of possession. Thinly spread across the north-eastern mountainside or, like my wife's family, living in a snug array of fields on the edge of Ballisodare Bay, the vitality of the Christian faith in which I had grown up was simply not there.

Except, that is, for my mother-in-law, though she found it difficult to express this in words. She was a woman of action, never more so than in preparation for church on a Sunday. There was always bustle. Somehow, the gathering together of the whole family ended in a rush to find hymn and prayer books, hats, sometimes flowers for the altar, and then getting everyone into the car and minding the turn onto the road, and the sharp bend at the Sandy Field. In spite of this very Protestant sense of urgency and direction, she always had about her a climate of calm and inspiring faith, and from her I learned a great deal about goodness and truthfulness.

We sat at the front of the church. The harmonium, played by Mrs Carter, was sustained in its uncertainty by our assured voices. The congregation kept things going, musically speaking. Dean Brown kept things in order spiritually.

My experiences, then and later, taught me that the Church to which I now belonged was not outspoken or assertive. Yet I was; and I became more so with the passage of time. I felt that the assertion of faith was much more important than any need to identify oneself through membership of a Church. I saw the importance of this for others, but I saw it also as an exclusive and limiting approach. The Church of Ireland might be small, I reasoned, but it had an authority that derived from its integrity. And for me there was the added reality of the faith. It made complete sense.

I belong now to a large Dublin parish, St Paul's in Glenageary. I share closely the views of its rector, Archdeacon Gordon Linney, and I admire particularly his courage and outspokenness. His views are always tempered by great charity.

I find the expression of my own faith most easily exercised through the Eucharist and go to early service most Sundays where I assist when needed and read the Epistle. We follow the *Book of*

Common Prayer at that early morning service and I love its language and its form. The Collects through the year include many of the most perfect prayers ever written.

Prayer is a problem in the modern Church, whatever the denomination. The attempts to make the place and the event "enjoyable" and friendly for those participating has introduced too much action and not enough contemplation. Prayer needs stillness and composure and reflection. The shape of the Communion service helps towards this. The prayers are not just beautiful in themselves; they encapsulate the very kernel of our faith, in the Prayer of Humble Access, "We do not presume . . ."

We Protestants value two sacraments, not seven. When I was baptised I conducted my own defence, steadfastly stated my belief and in return heard and accepted the priest's description of what this meant. Then I was confirmed.

The Communion Service that I regularly attend is from the *Book of Common Prayer*, as it was then. I have a clear memory of the feelings and of the atmosphere of those many Sundays. I recall rising early, hurrying up to chapel on the hill at school in the Cotswolds through sunlight or through snow, and continuing in what has been a lifelong desire to understand the particular mysteries of the Protestant faith. Belonging to the Church of Ireland has restored in me much of the certainty of early religious experience. I see this as a blessing on my existence, an enrichment of all that I attempt to do.

Rachel Bewley Bateman

Rachel M. Bewley Bateman is a former Clerk of Ireland Yearly Meeting and Elder of Dublin Monthly Meeting of the Religious Society of Friends (Quakers). Daughter of Victor E.H. and M. Winifred Bewley she attended Rathgar Junior School, Dublin and Newtown School, Waterford. She is a former Director of Bewleys Cafes Ltd. and J&R Bateman Textiles Ltd. She is  *currently a member of the Irish School of Ecumenics Trust Council.*

I was born to Quaker parents in Dublin in 1943, the second of three girls. For two years we had a foster-brother who came from Bergen-Belsen concentration camp after the Second World War. Through this early experience we learned something of the effects of war and how fortunate we were not to have suffered as others had done.

We attended Quaker schools in Dublin and Waterford. My father had been sent to a Quaker boarding school in York, England, but my parents felt it more appropriate that we should be educated in the country in which we were living. We enjoyed our schooldays. We were happy to have Jewish classmates, but Roman Catholic children were encountered mostly on the hockey or rugby pitches. Our parents invited overseas students and travelling Quakers to our home so we learned to appreciate both diversity and the world family of Friends (Quakers) from an early age. There have been both Quakers and Bewleys in Ireland for nearly 350 years. Family holidays were, and still are, spent in Connemara.

I have always been happy and proud to be Irish, but during my schooldays I did have a feeling that there was a degree of

Irishness to be obtained only if you were Irish and Roman Catholic. This view came from the terminology used in Irish language texts, the Irish history curriculum and Irish culture. I know the words of our national anthem in two languages, but as a pacifist I was uncomfortable with them.

While I was studying hotel management in the Dublin College of Catering, the staff went out of their way to ensure that the two Quaker students were happy. We enjoyed the opportunity to exchange views with our Catholic colleagues. There followed a year in France and Switzerland to gain experience in the catering trade. I later worked for three years as assistant warden in the Friends International Centre in London, where we created a home-from-home for visitors and students of well over 50 nationalities. I thoroughly enjoyed meeting so many interesting people. In 1967, I represented the Irish Quakers at the Friends World Conference in North Carolina, USA. Travelling from London with a plane-load of international Quakers was a unique experience, which was followed by a month of Quaker encounters and hospitality in the USA and Canada. I also visited Eastern Europe in 1965, 1983 and 1988. I spent two years in the Selly Oak Colleges in Birmingham, the first in Woodbrooke Quaker Study Centre and the second working in Fircroft (a working men's college).

I returned home in 1969 to work in the family business, but with the idea in my mind that, because of the *Ne Temere* decree and the small number of Quakers, I would probably not marry in Ireland. I had already been using visits home to bring contraceptives to a married couple. Their use was not against my conscience or theirs, but contraceptives could not be purchased in Ireland at that time.

At this point I must stress that we, as Quakers, consider ourselves to be Christians, neither Protestant nor Catholic. Personally, I am happy to be a non-conformist. As such, this has provided opportunities and opened doors. The folk memory of what Quakers did in Ireland during the 1840s famine years has also enhanced our reputation in society. I feel that this brings responsibilities also. Quakers have been successful in business. Our commitment to the one standard of truth has earned us the right to "affirm" rather than swear in a court of law. Quakers were, until recently, specifically mentioned in the Irish Constitution. We have been invited by government ministers to explain our point of view on divorce, abortion, and other matters. My father was appointed official adviser to the Minister for the Environment in relation to Travellers. Few Quakers have gone into politics, but our belief in the value of each human being, and in particular our Peace Testimony, encourages us to practise what we preach.

My involvement in Quaker peace and service activities led to my becoming a founder member of the Glencree Centre for Reconciliation and also a member of the Northern Ireland Committee for Quaker Peace and Service. We co-operated with Pax-Christi and other peace groups, participating in peace marches and quiet personal contacts with individuals and representatives across the political spectrum. The first Glencree Council was deliberately drawn from members of various religious denominations. This gave us a wide range of contacts in both Northern and southern Ireland. We brought a variety of experience and viewpoints to both our deliberations and work. We learned a great deal and did what we could, always conscious that County Wicklow was a long way from the first-hand experiences of people in Northern Ireland.

At this time I was working in Bewleys Cafés and really appreciated the opportunity to get to know fellow Dubliners, both staff and customers. Bewleys became a common-ownership company and we changed from waitress service to self-service in the restaurants. The firm's Jersey cows were exhibited at the Royal Dublin Society Spring Show in Ballsbridge, where family members were regular visitors.

John Bateman and I were married in 1984. He was a member of the Church of Ireland from West Cork. We consciously developed our joint commitment to both Quaker and Church of Ireland communities, while also embracing other ecumenical activities. On one occasion, he and I processed up the aisle together with the priests of the Dublin Archdiocese for the consecration of two Roman Catholic Bishops. We had front row seats and over three hours in which to develop our understanding of Roman Catholic liturgy! We have valued our local inter-faith fellowship and are fortunate in the number of different Churches represented in our area, as well as both Orthodox and Progressive Jewish syna-gogues. This year there were also Muslim speakers in two local churches.

I have been happy to represent Friends (Quakers) on a variety of ecumenical occasions at both national and local level and have been involved with the religious element of the inauguration of two Presidents of Ireland. On the last occasion, we addressed the fact that Ireland is becoming an increasingly multi-faith commu-nity. I have found in the Irish School of Ecumenics a valuable re-source for developing thought on a range of topical issues.

We in Ireland have plenty to contribute as well as learn. We are fortunate to live in a beautiful country. We should cherish our diversity and help to create a better environment for all. We are Irish, European and inhabitants of a small planet called Earth. Can we learn to share more of what we have and support others in time of need?

Phyllis Browne

Phyllis Harrison was born in 1920. Raised in a Protestant household in Dublin, she was an introspective child who developed a great passion for music and art. In 1936, she met and fell in love with Dr Noel Browne, one of the most respected and radical politicians of his generation. They spent over 60 years of marriage together before his death in 1997. Throughout their marriage, Phyllis stood firmly by her husband during his tussle with  *the Roman Catholic hierarchy over his Mother and Child Scheme and is still tigerishly defensive of his good name. Her memoirs of their life together,* Thanks for the tea, Mrs Browne, *were published in 1998. Forever a pacifist, a humanist and a lady committed to her husband's happiness, now aged 82, she lives in Connemara alone, but with many good friends.*

"Gilt-edged Bibles in our Gloved Hands . . ."

It is an interesting and accepted fact that quite young children, on hearing a snippet of conversation between adults, can worry, often unnecessarily, about what they have heard, until in time they can reason and understand. Uncertainties and problems abound in their lonely heads.

As a very young child I was certain of only one thing: I was one of six children in a family labelled "Protestant"; this made me feel very different from all the other children of the neighbourhood. With my sister and young brother we soon realised why we felt different; it was because we *were* different. We even looked different, especially on Sundays.

Sunday was a serious day, to be spent quietly wearing our Sunday clothes, "not for vanity", as we were constantly reminded, but to please the Lord! My mother, clever with the needle, would have spent time during the week at her sewing machine so that my sister and I would have something new to wear to church. Well-polished shoes of patent leather, ankle-strapped, with ribbons and flowers on a hat and white lace gloves to finish the outfit. Aunts, friends and cousins would call to keep mother company during her sewing evening. I would hear them chatting away with stories of their church and family matters — whose daughter was keeping company with a Roman Catholic boy, what family was in financial trouble, etc. I understood little of the gossip, but knew it was serious to these Protestant churchgoers, and it worried me.

Sunday mornings were spent at Sunday school where, for an hour or more, we listened to how to behave "when we go out into the world", the meaning of New Testament stories, verses of the psalms, and singing of hymns. Later we attended the "Morning Service" and Holy Communion, in our parish church. Extremely hungry, we reached home to enjoy the roast beef and Yorkshire pudding followed by mother's sweet.

Our Roman Catholic friends spent a different sort of day. They would go to the cinema, a football match, take a train trip to Bray; their interest in Church services was almost nil. But they were interested as we walked along the pathway, when they noticed our gilt-edged bibles in our gloved hands — "Proddy, Proddy on the wall, half a loaf would feed you all" they would chant as we passed, utterly embarrassed. My young brother, a choirboy in St Patrick's Cathedral, had to wear an "Eton" suit, so uncomfortable with its stiff white collar, bow tie and waistcoat. He went to the service on his bicycle, hoping not to get noticed, covered with scarf and cap.

These small trifles of worry, when we think of them now, are pathetic, yet I suppose they had some sort of effect on our characters. We felt that we were looked down upon by the newly formed "Republic" when, in the early 1920s, the Civil War was fought. We were still looked upon as "British", even though we were as Irish as any Roman Catholic, except for religious belief.

The Roman Catholic hierarchy now saw their opportunity to take over the education of the new State, teaching their people to eventually take over all aspects of life — health, religious affairs, the laws and business in general. Just one newspaper, *The Irish Times*, at that time, perhaps still, took a different view; their advertisements in the "Situations Vacant" column almost always added, "Protestants only need apply". In truth, I expect that both religions are to blame for our state of affairs, though the rules of the Roman Catholics, I feel, concentrate more on man's ideas of what is right or wrong, while Protestant ways are more simple, and follow the teachings of Jesus in the New Testament. The Roman Catholic hierarchy's undemocratic interference in State affairs has done great harm to the progress of the country. Church and State should be separate; there might be peace if this were so, for it is a mistake to think that to be a "Roman Catholic" is the same as to be a "Christian".

One of the cleverest ideas of the Roman Catholic hierarchy was to introduce the *Ne Temere* decree. It was possibly the final reason for the almost complete disappearance of the Church of Ireland congregations. With a small population, the number of suitable young men for young Protestant girls to marry were becoming fewer and fewer.

The *Ne Temere* decree was a promise in a mixed marriage that all the children would be brought up in the Roman Catholic faith. Some couples of course did not keep their promise, but this could bring trouble from the local priest, who would call to the house and argue with the children's parents. Our two daughters were sometimes treated unfairly in school, being looked upon as half Roman Catholic and half Protestant. I must have changed their school at least five times, but never found nuns who would be pleasant to them. To my surprise, even a well-known Protestant school refused to take them. So, as time went by, Roman Catholics became better educated as Protestants became fewer. There were fewer jobs for them, and many emigrated. Each of my four brothers, my sister, and many close relations, well educated and clever, would have preferred to live and work in their own country, but after some years trying to find suitable employment they reluctantly had to emigrate. This breaking of the family was distressing for my parents, who forever waited for the postman. But there was no alternative; the few suitable jobs for Protestants were already filled. Sadly, my brothers and their families, when forced to emigrate, got caught up in the war in the Far East. Many miserable years were spent imprisoned by the Japanese.

Most young children learn without understanding; they singsong their Church's teachings as they do their multiplication tables. However, something happens one day when they are a little older, something they remember forever, something that forces them to understand.

My sister and I enjoyed our Saturday afternoons attending gymnastics and dancing classes run by Miss Pemberton in our local parish hall. In neat clothes, white socks and soft white shoes, we were a happy bunch, and won many medals in the Girl's Brigade competitions, to the excellent accompaniment of the patient Miss Tisdale on piano. She did not seem to mind how many times she was asked to repeat the same few bars of music over and over until Miss Pemberton was happy with our efforts.

One Saturday afternoon, we noticed Miss Pemberton in an unpleasant disagreement with the parish curate, head of the church and the school hall that we used. He heard that a Roman Catholic girl had joined the classes. He refused to allow this, and ordered immediate disbandment of the classes.

Miss Pemberton refused to give up, believing that no child should be treated differently because she was brought up in a faith not everyone agreed with. So, bravely, the teacher kept her group together for many years, finding different suitable halls where necessary — The Railway Union Hall, The Damer Hall and a dark old hall off Capel Street.

This behaviour, I learned, was bigotry on the part of the supposed Christian churchman. For the first time I realised that being a different faith could indeed be a worrying matter; I was quite angry that one of my own Church could be so narrow-minded and un-Christian.

This story is long in the past, and now, as a very old lady, I can see that many changes have taken place, some good, some bad, certainly not enough and at too high a price. Greed and desire for power and property appears to me to still run through our community, though power of course can be a good thing if used for the betterment of society.

Living according to the Ten Commandments, loving our neighbours as ourselves, would surely do away with the troubles we visit upon ourselves — war, hunger, deprivation of all kinds. Everyone's wish is for peace with justice. Do we need another 2,000 years to reach that goal?

Robin Bury

Robin Bury was born in 1940 in Nagpur, India of an Irish father and Canadian mother. He attended Midleton College, County Cork, from 1948–53, St Columba's College, Dublin from 1953–58 and Trinity College Dublin from 1958–63. He received a degree in Modern History and Political Science and a Higher Diploma in Education (Hons). He worked for Córas Tráchtála, the Irish Export Board, from 1971–78 based in London, Dublin and Canada. From 1978–2001 he was Export Manager in Antigen Pharmaceuticals, Roscrea, and Senior Executive in Jacobs Biscuits, Dublin. In 2001, he was Chairman of the Reform Movement, which represents the old minority in the south and works for pluralism.

"There May be Consequences"

My parents moved from Nagpur, in the heartland of India, to Skibbereen in the isolated south-west of Ireland in 1948. My Dad had been a padre in the British army and we had lived in a spacious, colonial-style bungalow with servants. We went to a cold draughty house outside Skibbereen with neither running water nor electricity. Why we moved there is a mystery, most especially to my mother, a bright witty Canadian who was most at home in a large city. Perhaps it had something to do with Dad's ancestors, West Brits who once owned Little Island in lovely Cork Harbour, where they built two Georgian houses, one a mansion, both now levelled. Or perhaps it was second choice after the parish in the North he had failed to get.

I grew up in an Ireland where the Protestant community had "collapsed", in the words of Marcus Tanner in *Ireland's Holy Wars*. Numbers had declined from 440,000 in 1861 to some 150,000 in 1948 and 100,000 by 1996. There was a huge exodus in 1920–24 during a period of cleansing by the IRA, when some 90,000 fled. In the Ireland where we settled, de Valera's 1937 sectarian Constitution had alienated the dwindling population further with the bleak message that "No Protestants need apply", in the blunt words of Noel Browne in his book *Against the Tide*. Many of the children of those who chose to stay were subjected to the *Ne Temere* decree, imposed by a triumphalist Catholic Church to ensure that the children in mixed religion marriages were raised as Catholics.

I was sent to an austere boys' school, Midleton College, County Cork, at the age of eight. An early memory was outside the twelfth-century Norman cathedral in Cloyne, east Cork, where my father had become the Dean. Cloyne is nothing more than a crossroads but is famous as the birthplace of both Bishop Berkeley and Christy Ring. I collected my bicycle from the sexton's shed in the cathedral grounds every day when coming home from school. Local Catholics crossed themselves when passing the cathedral, which I found strange, the property being in the hands of heretical Protestants. I was about to be enlightened. One afternoon as I approached the gate leading to the footpath in front of the cathedral, the parish priest suddenly appeared and closed the little gate in my face. He had been waiting for me. While holding his hand on the gate, he told me that I had no right to be there, that the cathedral was stolen property and I should tell my father of this dastardly deed when I got home. Terrified, I pedalled home pronto to pass on this devastating news. To my relief, my father laughed and said the cathedral had been offered to the Catholic Church in the past, as the upkeep was too expensive for the mere 100 or so parishioners to meet. But unfortunately there had been no interest, theft and all considered.

My parents were monarchists. Every Sunday in Cloyne Cathedral, my Dad prayed for the British sovereign, as well as the

President of Ireland. A local landed gentleman, Mr de Vere, who mostly lived in London and sent his children to English public schools, became increasingly disturbed at my father's wayward behaviour. But as far as my Dad was concerned, the Church of Ireland was just that: the Church of the island of Ireland. The Queen was sovereign in the North and the Irish President was head of State in the south, so he prayed for both of them.

Eventually, Mr de Vere was invited to dinner in the deanery to discuss his concerns. He was worried, he said, that "there might be consequences". Perhaps he was scared that his converted stable-yard house would be burnt down, his castle having met such a fate in the 1920s. East Cork was, after all, a strong republican area from which thousands of Protestants had fled. I was called down to give my opinion. Of course, I readily supported my parents, and would so today, believing that we should have settled for home rule and never left the UK, never mind the Commonwealth. Shortly after this dinner, the Queen's name did not get mentioned as frequently in my father's prayers, but this was more to comply with the synod's directions than the anxieties of our neighbour. Not long after, Mr de Vere left Ireland for good. It was not the IRA that did for him but the Land Commission, which had seen off many a Protestant landowner.

I married a Catholic whom I met and fell in love with at Trinity College, Dublin. This could have caused my father huge difficulties, were it not for the fact that my wife, Geraldine Reidy, had left her Church in protest at its attitudes to feminist issues. She worshipped in the cathedral when visiting Cloyne. However, difficulties arose when we decided to get married. At that time, the Catholic Church insisted on people in mixed religion marriages getting married not only in a Catholic Church, but at a side altar therein, preferably early in the morning when no one was around to witness the ceremony. Prods, after all could not get into heaven. I had to take the *Ne Temere* decree. The kindly Dublin priest told me it was a "gentleman's agreement" and I replied that it was one to which my wife and I would not be paying too much attention. He did not seem to care as long as I signed the document promising to bring up all our children as Catholics. I need not have worried about breaking what was disputably a legal agreement, as Geraldine insisted that our three children be brought up in the Church of Ireland. But because of the humiliation that my Dad would have suffered as a result of our having to get married at a side altar, we went to liberal, pagan England. There, not only were we made to feel warmly welcomed at the main altar, but my father was invited to say prayers with the priest during the wedding ceremony.

I have spent all of my working life promoting Irish exports, first in Córas Tráchtála (CTT), later in private companies. I recall an incident which illustrates a degree of sectarianism in the old CTT, an organisation I loved. In 1973, some time after my Dad died, the diocese of Cloyne had been amalgamated with the neighbouring Midleton parish and the title of Dean had been moved to Midleton, Protestant numbers having fallen so drastically in Cloyne diocese. One day I came to work and an Assistant Chief Executive in CTT was waiting to give me this news, which of course I knew about already. He was clearly pleased and wanted my reaction. I told him that this was the story of most Protestant parishes in Ireland since 1922, and that many Protestants had left to work in England and elsewhere, including those with whom I had been to school and university. Many of the children of those who stayed behind had been subjected to the *Ne Temere* decree. I added that the cathedral was full of Catholics at my father's funeral service, an example of true Christianity in Ireland. He was somewhat taken aback by my frankness and thereafter my career, which had been advancing well, came to a standstill. A colleague noticing this, but not knowing the cause, courageously tried to intervene, but got nowhere. I left CTT a few years later to pursue a career in the private sector.

Hubert Butler, the acclaimed essayist, believed that Protestants should play a strong part in their communities by bringing to bear the essential Protestant free-thinking spirit, individualistic, rebellious and mistrustful, even "vilifying the State", in Butler's own words. I would agree, but first the self-confidence of one of the world's most talented minorities needs to be revived.

As for Protestant Church leaders, too often moral cowardice parades as diplomacy in the pursuit of ecumenism, which has ended in rejection and humiliation. There is no heart for promoting the beliefs and the ethics of the democratic, Reformed Churches. W.B. Yeats was the last senator to protest at the imposition of Catholic-inspired legislation on his "people". Today, Protestant leaders like Archbishops Empey and Eames and Protestant senators willingly acquiesce in RTE broadcasting the Angelus bell, the only public service broadcaster in Europe to do this. They did not support David Trimble when he pointed out the obvious: the Irish State is monocultural and monoethnic. In the new more secular Ireland, where the sun has set on Catholic nationalist triumphalism, more positive leadership is essential to revive Protestant confidence. And, if it is serious about unity, the Irish State needs to start this process now.

Note: The name de Vere is fictitious in order to protect the family, whose members are living outside Ireland.

Archbishop Donald Caird

The Most Reverend Dr Donald A.R. Caird, BA, MA, BD, HDipEd, is former Archbishop of Dublin and Glendalough and Primate of Ireland. Born in Dublin in 1925, he was educated privately and at Wesley College Dublin (1935-44), and Trinity College Dublin (1944–50). He was curate in Dundela, Belfast (1950–53); assistant master and chaplain at Portora Royal School, Enniskillen (1953–57); rector at Rathmichael Parish church, Shankill (1960); assistant master at St Columba's College, Dublin (1960–67); deputy lecturer in philosophy at TCD (1962–63); and Dean of Ossory (1969–70). He was Bishop of Limerick, Ardfert and Aghadoe (1970–76) and of Meath and Kildare (1976–85), and was elected Archbishop of Dublin in 1985. He has been awarded a number of honorary degrees, the latest being a PhD awarded in 2002 by the Pontifical University, St Patrick's College, Maynooth. He is chairman or member of the boards of a number of organisations, including The Church of Ireland Theological College Management Committee, the Commission for the Care of the Elderly, the Governors of Marsh's Library, the Rotunda Hospital and Tallaght Hospital (President). He is also a patron of a number of hospitals and schools.

The requirement to write an essay of 1,000 words on the theme of my experience as a Church of Ireland citizen of the Republic of Ireland has concentrated my mind and energised my memory in a way that the prospect of immediate hanging is reputed to do by Dr Samuel Johnson.

I was born at the end of 1925 in Dublin when the country was just emerging from a prolonged period of conflict and civil unrest: a World War from 1914 to 1918; a Rebellion largely in Dublin in 1916; a War of Independence from 1919 to 1921; a Civil War from

1921 to 1923. A large part of the central city lay in ruins, emotions were tender and suspicions were rife.

The community into which I was born, Dublin middle-class Church of Ireland, was uncertain of its future, so uncertain in fact that in May 1922, at a meeting of the Synod in Dublin, John Gregg, the Archbishop of Dublin, had led a deputation from the Synod Hall to Dáil Éireann to ask whether the new State wished the Protestant community to leave the State or stay. In his famous "part and parcel" speech, Kevin O'Higgins, on behalf of the Dáil, gave generous assurances to the Protestant citizens of the new State that the Protestant community would not only be welcome to stay but that they would be especially appreciated in participation in the life of the nation. John Gregg accepted this promise and tacitly encouraged members of the Church of Ireland to stay and to contribute to the full of their capacity to the life of the new State in all its aspects. By his own commitment, by his forthright and constructive criticism of the policies of the government, by his presentation and defence of the new State to the Anglican world in which his opinions held considerable sway world-wide, he gave courageous and unmistakable leadership to the Church of Ireland community and assuaged many of their qualms.

The promise made by Kevin O'Higgins on behalf of Dáil Éireann was honoured insofar as it was possible for the State to do so. There were incidents of murder, intimidation and destruction of property and considerable anecdotal evidence of local harassment of Protestant families in isolated parts of the country. But these incidents were recognised as largely the work of criminal opportunist elements, or of the small percentage of the populace who awaited any occasion to cause trouble, but they did not constitute an organised vendetta against a largely defenceless Protestant community.

Archbishop John Gregg continued as Archbishop of Dublin throughout the formative years of the Irish Free State, making a valuable contribution to the composition of the 1937 Constitution. The Archbishop and the Taoiseach, Eamon de Valera, bore a striking resemblance to one another, both in physical appearance and in their cautious scholarly approach to the resolution of questions presented to them. They enjoyed considerable rapport and mutual respect. This personal relationship eased any tension that arose in negotiations with the State over such issues as the introduction of compulsory Irish into the education programme in 1926 and the course for the training of teachers for primary schools. Dr Gregg's influence was formative in determining the attitude of the great majority of the Protestants to the new State, which was to be accepting, loyal and cautiously critical.

The years of the Second World War seemed to deepen the separation and isolation of the two States into which Ireland was divided since 1920, Northern Ireland and the Irish Free State. They drifted further apart. Little or no initiative to effect co-operation or reconciliation was forthcoming at national level on either side and in the vacuum suspicion and animosity grew. The General Synod of the Church of Ireland continued to meet in Dublin as it had done since 1870 and gave assuring and indeed impressive evidence of the unity of the Church of Ireland in face of the division of the country. It was possible for strong unionists and members of the Orange Order to sit beside men and women who had taken part in the Rebellion of 1916 and the Civil War and who had suffered imprisonment for their activities at the opening service of the General Synod and to have debated together on issues important to the Church of Ireland on the floor of the Synod. Political divisions did not destroy the unity of the Church which transcended them.

The two most significant events to occur in Ireland during my lifetime affecting both Church and State, events whose effects are ongoing and whose final outcome we have not yet seen, are the economic revolution in the Republic of Ireland brought about in the late 1950s and 1960s by the brilliant co-operation of the then Taoiseach, Sean Lemass, and the Secretary of the Department of Finance, Dr Kenneth Whitaker; and the coming after the Second Vatican Council in 1966 of the ecumenical movement to Ireland.

Relations between the Republic of Ireland and Northern Ireland came to life through the initiative of Sean Lemass, a veteran

of the Rebellion and the Civil War, but at heart a Dublin busi-
nessman, and Dr Kenneth Whitaker, a practical economist who
dealt with the daily financial business of the nation, who saw
clearly through the welter of myths of emotion which clouded the
relationship between North and south.

The pragmatic, non-doctrinaire initiative, unburdened by
much of the baggage of history, which Sean Lemass and Kenneth
Whitaker took to encourage the government of Northern Ireland
to join in the discussion of projects which would benefit the economic position of both parts of Ireland found a wide response in
the hard-headed Northern community under the leadership of the
Prime Minister, Terence O'Neill, a lord of ancient Irish lineage.
Exchange visits were made between the Prime Minister and the
Taoiseach; the fruits of this rapprochement spilled over into many
other areas of the life of both States besides the immediate focus of
trade and economics; a real opening up of hearts and minds was
revealed and great hopes were entertained for the peace and
prosperity of the whole country. Sadly, this rapprochement did
not suit political and religious elements whose vested interest in
discord and violence was threatened by it and they soon engi-
neered the collapse of the Stormont Government under O'Neill
and brought the process of rapprochement to a temporary end.
But the economic revolution continued with great success in the
Republic of Ireland, bringing a period of unprecedented growth
and prosperity over the next 20 to 30 years.

The other event was the arrival of the ecumenical movement
in Ireland at the conclusion of the Second Vatican Council in 1966.
The ecumenical movement had been on the road since the International Missionary Conference in Edinburgh in 1910. It had survived two World Wars and innumerable other setbacks before
resulting in the formation of the World Council of Churches in
1948, which involved Reformed Churches representing
480,000,000 Christians seeking a form of unity consistent with
their common Christian faith and drawing closer together to show
Christian solidarity to meet the challenge of all the problems and
evils which the world presents — poverty, disease, racial factions,

etc. So far, the World Council of Churches, with its massive head-quarters in Geneva, was the most tangible expression of ecumenism until Pope John XXIII boldly led the Roman Catholic Church into the van of the movement, to the great joy of Christendom, or at least most parts of it. Long pent-up expressions of Christian fellowship burst forth; in the case of Anglicans, with the visit of the Archbishop of Canterbury to Pope Paul VI, when the Pope referred to the Anglican and Roman Catholic Churches as too-long separated sisters, and each committed himself to seeking on the basis of their common faith a deeper unity in truth and love. Those were days of euphoria; slower and more cautious days have followed, as we were led to expect, on the principle that large bodies move slowly and the Churches in the ecumenical movement are large bodies. But it is now nearly 40 years since the documents of the Second Vatican Council were published and Joint Commissions were set up to examine common grounds of faith and doctrine and to report to their principals, the major world Churches in ecumenical dialogue, on ways to effect closer unity on the grounds of common belief and doctrine.

In most cases, these Joint Commissions, like ARCIC (The Anglican–Roman Catholic International Commission) produced its final report more than 20 years ago. In some cases, second generation commissions have been established to clarify elements in the reports of the first commissions, and even to examine new material. There seems to be no logical end to this process, so that generation after generation of Christians in all our Churches must endure what the *Book of Common Prayer* refers to as "our unhappy divisions".

Our hope and prayer must be for effective action by the Churches involved in ecumenical dialogue at the highest level to bring in that unity for which Christ prayed in the Great High Priestly Prayer in the Gospel according to St John, chapter 17, verse 21: *"ut omnes unum sint"* — "that they all may be one". That is a unity which would make all our other divisions trivial.

❧ ❧ ❧

Harold Clarke

Harold Clarke was born in Castlecoote, County Roscommon, in 1932 and educated in The King's Hospital, Dublin and in TCD, where he read Economics and Political Science. He joined Eason & Son Ltd. in 1954 and was appointed Chairman of the Board in 1986, a position he held until his retirement in 1995. He has written a number of books about Ireland and was commissioning editor of The Irish Heritage Series of booklets. He was a pioneer in the restoration of Georgian Dublin when he undertook the refurbishment of a derelict 1787 house in North Great George's Street. Since retirement, he has created a 3½-acre garden in Avoca, County Wicklow.

Memories of a Protestant Boyhood

Memory has a knack of being selective but mine is not playing tricks when I recall a happy and fulfilled childhood. It must be admitted that to be Protestant in the south in the middle of the last century was in most cases to be privileged to a greater or lesser extent. It was a time when the children of most of our neighbours had to emigrate to survive, probably never to return, and it was also a time when I knew whole families wiped out by tuberculosis, or consumption as it was then known.

So what was it like being Protestant in an overwhelmingly Catholic society? For a start, we never doubted our Irishness. We might not play or support Gaelic football but that was just one aspect of being Irish and I have never in earlier or later years had my Irishness challenged because of being Protestant. After all, the then President of Ireland came from our community and our county and nobody doubted his Irishness. This was a time when people were identified less by positives than negatives: Protestants were people who did not play games or work on Sunday, Catholics were those who did not eat meat on Friday, and so on. Only after Vatican II did we start thinking of the positives and what we had in common.

I was born in 1932, the year of the Eucharistic Congress, in which the marriage of the newly independent State and the triumphalist Catholic Church was solemnised. I was the youngest of six children, five boys and one girl; my father's family would be what are known as "strong farmers" in County Roscommon. There were no records of when the family arrived there but it seems likely that they were Cromwellians who joined the Gaelic Irish in preferring to go to Connacht rather than the alternative. They were certainly established in Castlecoote, home of the Gunning sisters of legendary beauty, in the middle of the eighteenth century. My mother's family farmed in the Ards Peninsula in County Down.

The Clarkes were Church of Ireland but my mother came from a Presbyterian family and my father's mother was a Methodist, so although we conformed to the once established Church there were influences which made us aware of the wider range of Reformation Churches. Each Sunday we would attend Donamon church and one Sunday each month proceed to the Methodist church in Roscommon, which had been built by my grandmother when she arrived as a bride from Banbridge. On another Sunday each month we would attend the Presbyterian church. The service in Donamon on one Sunday in the month would be Evening Prayer followed by Holy Communion, with an interval between to allow children and other non-participants to withdraw, and on other Sundays it was Evening Prayer according to the *Book of Common Prayer*. Whether for office or sacrament, the rector was similarly vested in surplice, BA hood and black scarf. When the bishop visited, he would also wear a cassock. The church was without ornamentation other than the splendiferous marble tablets to the Caulfield family with their over-the-top tributes, which relieved many a long sermon. The altar, always referred to as the communion table, was covered in a drab wine-coloured frontal, which must be the only colour that has no place in any liturgical rota. Then, as now, I could not understand the appeal of this variety of low-Church Anglicanism which I have seldom found in other parts of the world but is still encountered in some parts of the Republic and in many parishes in Northern Ireland. It is interesting that liturgical renewal and television worship has had a marked influence in the south but has left the North almost completely untouched. Over half a century later, Christ Church Cathedral, Dublin, is arguably the most interesting place of worship from the liturgical point of view in the entire country.

As a child, attending Catholic funerals of neighbours, with their mysterious Latin prayers and wafting incense, seemed so exotic by comparison. We would join the wrinkled men at the back of the chapel who knelt on one knee on their caps, providing a buffer from the cold stone.

A few generations before, pre *Ne Temere*, there had been a second marriage in our family outside the faith, which gave us kinsfolk locally who were Roman Catholics. Interestingly, both we and they were proud of the connection and we would socialise on any suitable occasion. Tragically, the new marriage rules introduced at the turn of the twentieth century created a barrier between the two religions that we are only now recovering from.

Our education was begun with a governess whom we shared with the local doctor's children and the boys in due course attended the local Catholic national school, as there was no other. The head teacher had a huge respect for Protestants and claimed that he had never been told a lie by one of them. This widespread belief in the superior integrity of Protestants was to suffer a body blow in the 1990s when several large farmers from the community were jailed for feeding growth promoters to their cattle, and the integrity was further questioned in recent times when Protestant names appeared among the Ansbacher depositors.

We had to leave the classroom during religious instruction (although I can still recite the Hail Mary and the Angelus!), which was given just before lunch each day, giving a privilege denied to the other pupils. In the summer, most children would come to school barefoot, which many would regard as an economic indicator but in fact it was more a cultural practice which probably originated in poverty but was later accepted as normal.

Relations with those who worked on the farm were an important influence when growing up. In many cases, there were marriages between the domestic staff and farm workers and thus a dynasty of loyalty was established, with support being given in both directions, and this loyalty could continue for generations.

My father and his brother had been sent to Woodhouse Grove, a small public school in Yorkshire, as was the fashion of the day. There in pre-racist days they were known as Pat Primus and Pat Secundus. They finished there on the outbreak of the First World War and my father was sent to the Ranelagh School for boys in Athlone, which his father had also attended. The school was closed in the 1930s and became the Gentex factory. The late Brian Lenihan told me that there was some local pressure to remove the Arms of the Earl of Ranelagh from the pediment but his father refused on the grounds that they were part of the history of the building. The Ranelagh School for girls in Roscommon was closed down earlier and my grandparents moved there in 1919. My mother was educated in The Lodge, Fortwilliam Park in Belfast, a fairly short-lived academy for young ladies which had as its main claim to fame that Helen Waddell, the chronicler of Heloise and Abelard, was a teacher there. When it came to sending their children to boarding school, my parents could not fall back on any family tradition. The King's Hospital in Dublin was chosen, a place of incredible austerity even for its day in the 1940s. Its ethos and practice was strictly and uncompromisingly Anglican. The Headmaster/Chaplain, J.J. Butler, had been a curate in All Saints, Grangegorman, a church with a mildly Tractarian tradition, so chapel was a much more colourful affair than we were accustomed to. Moving from Roscommon pan-Protestantism to *Missa de Angelis* on Sunday mornings was a change indeed. To be in the Head's good books, one had to excel at cricket or sing in the choir. I achieved half of this and got by.

Bishop Richard Clarke

The Right Reverend Richard Clarke was born in 1949 in Dublin. His secondary school education was at Wesley College Dublin; he attended Trinity College, Dublin, and King's College London, holding a doctorate from the former. He was ordained into the Church of Ireland ministry in Holywood, County Down, in 1975. He ministered also in Dublin and Cork prior to his appointment as Bishop of Meath and Kildare in 1996. He is married to Linda, a teacher. They have two children, Nicholas, a medical doctor, and Lindsey, a medical student in TCD. He is the author of a recent book on Christian theology, And Is It True?

Having reached the age of 53 in the summer of 2002, I find myself able (not entirely without a sense of shock) to look back over five decades of change and adaptation in the business of being what is simplistically termed a "Protestant" in the Republic of Ireland. It is of course dangerous to assume that each period of ten years — particularly as summed up by the title of the decade (*the fifties, the sixties* and so forth) — will mark a specific culture or epoch. Strangely, however, I find this does more or less work as I look back on my life as a member of a minority Christian tradition, the Church of Ireland, living in the Irish Republic. Indeed, I was born a matter of weeks after the proclamation of the Irish Republic in 1949.

The word "apartheid" has unpleasant overtones, and yet it is hard to think of a Church of Ireland childhood in the 1950s, growing up in the north Dublin suburb of Drumcondra, as other than a form of denominational apartheid. It was, of course, an extremely benign and civilised apartheid. The word sectarianism may have had meaning in Fethard-on-Sea in the 1950s, but in north Dublin it was apartheid by mutual consent. Roman Catholics and members of the Church of Ireland would have treated each other with genuine courtesy, would have been good neighbours one to another, but the overwhelming sense was one of difference. We were different. The word "ecumenism" was still in the future in the Christian vernacular. I well remember my father (who was a Church of Ireland clergyman) and local Roman Catholic clergy as being on friendly terms, but there would not have been a spiritual sharing in any serious sense. Most of my close friends as a child would have been those whom I knew through the Church of Ireland parish or the parish national school.

The 1960s — beginning with the exhilaration of the Kennedy years, the excitement of the second Vatican Council, continuing on into the year of student revolt, 1968 (yes, I did go on demonstrations!), and concluding with the "conquest" of the moon in the following year — were a different matter. It seemed as if there were no problems that could not be solved, and solved by means other than force. It seemed as if the Church could become a unified force for good in the world. The Vatican Council reminded us that there was a Church beyond Ireland and a vision beyond local realities. It seemed as though, in Ireland, we had become part of a real world.

If one could define the 1960s in terms of *idealism*, albeit an idealism which was at times naïve, the 1970s began with a real sense of hope. I lived in the Republic of Ireland for only a couple of years of the 1970s. I graduated from Trinity College, spent a year teaching English in Iran, and then studied theology in London for three years. I was ordained for a Northern Irish Diocese and it was 1977 before I returned to Dublin. I well recall, on becoming chaplain of Trinity College in 1979, having left it eight years earlier, reflecting on how much was different in Dublin, in Trinity, and in the Church, and not only my own tradition. Much of my native city of Dublin was no longer a place to wander around on one's own at any hour of day or night, without fear of violence. The proportion of Church of Ireland students in TCD had shrunk to a tiny fraction of the 1971 ratio. "The Ban", imposed by the Roman Catholic Church on Catholic students entering the College, had been lifted only in 1970. The college had more than doubled in size during the 1970s, and had perhaps become more anonymous. But the Church at large was a richer, brighter place to be. In Trinity, the chaplains of the different traditions worked more closely with one another than with colleagues of their own tradition outside the college. It was a time when ecumenism was felt everywhere. It was seen as an unstoppable force. How wrong we were.

The 1980s were a time of great personal happiness for me, with a young family and a move to a large country parish in west Cork. Yet, looking back, it was a time when things did not move forward, either for the country or for the Church. The Thatcherite sense of society as an illusion seemed to grow, and to infect all around it. Violence in Northern Ireland took on a terrifying and fatalistic inevitability. No-one could argue that it was a prophetic age of any of the Churches. We seemed, for all the good will and fine words, to become more introspective. Materialism, inside the Church and through every part of Irish society, tainted us all.

Then came the 1990s. The Church — all the Churches — moved from a place at the centre of Irish life to becoming, in the eyes of many, a pariah. Ecumenism became secondary to survival, although it should have been the opposite. The Churches' failures — whether the running sore of Drumcree or the obscene instances of child abuse — became matters for sneering and contempt to the Ireland outside the pews. It was not a comfortable time to be seen as a Christian priest.

Yet somehow, I believe the Church may now be able to move into a new, invigorating, exciting and fruitful phase, as we enter a new century and a new Christian millennium. The illusions have gone, our own and other people's. If we are ready for realism, we have a rich future. It will be a future when the divisions between different Christian traditions will be seen as infinitesimal in comparison to that which unites us. The battle will be for the credibility of the Gospel rather than for the victory of one Church over another. The Church, in all its traditions, will in God's grace understand itself as having a greater aspiration than the continuation of its own power, and certainly a higher vision than its own survival.

Bishop Paul Colton

The Right Reverend Paul Colton was born in Derry in 1960 of a Dublin father and Wexford mother at a time when the family were living near the border in Donegal. They moved to Cork when he was two and he has always considered it to be home. When asked where he's from, he calls himself "a truly Irish synthesis". Four years at Ashton School in Cork were followed by two scholarship years at the Lester B. Pear-

son College of the Pacific in British Columbia. A law graduate of UCC, he worked in Lisburn, Belfast and Dublin following ordination in 1984. In 1999 he was elected Bishop of Cork, Cloyne and Ross and is the first Church of Ireland bishop to be a graduate of the National University of Ireland. Susan, his wife, also from Cork, is a primary school teacher. They have twin sons, Andrew and Adam, who are eight years old.

The contemporary Ireland of 2002, fashioned by an emerging pluralism of identities, energised by arrivals from other countries, foists on us a refreshing measure of bewilderment. This contemporary disorientation places a healthy interrogative over residual notions of an untainted ideology of Irishness. As a confident member of a minority, I feel secure in that place of puzzlement. More than ever, there is a sense that the quest for an Irish purity (once measured by one's surname and religious identity) is both futile and naïve.

I've always felt at home here, even though in my early years I was sensitive to signals from some who suggested (whether because of surname, religious denomination, school uniform or as we played hockey instead) I wasn't quite "the real thing". Within my own community there were a few, of course, who pined for a former belonging: as in other families, there was that older relative who was genuinely self-persuaded that the same programme broadcast on RTE became infinitely superior once transmitted by the BBC!

New questions of identity and the presence of greater numbers of emerging minorities make this feel comfortably home. The measure of our maturity will be how we value minorities of many varieties, while at the same time cherishing recognised majorities.

A visit to the war cemetery at Tilly-sur-Seulles in Normandy reinforced this sense of identity and led to an exploration of family history with my eight-year-old twin sons. I told them, "Some say the Coltons were at the Battle of Hastings and came to Ireland in the sixteenth century." Who knows?

Photos were poured out of a box at home: a great-grandfather in the Boer War, a grandfather who was in the King's African Rifles (and subsequently served in the LDF); great-aunt Jenny, from Ballyvourney, who was a cook in the Auxiliary Territorial Service in the Second World War. (That last piece of knowledge ricocheted when we were looking at the photos in the museum at Bayeux of the D-Day landings. "Where's Jenny on the beach?" asked one of the boys.)

Family certificates read like a Dublin gazetteer: Westland Row, Irishtown, Portobello Barracks, Aungier Street, Havelock Terrace, Rosary Gardens and Blackrock. There's a plaque presented by Guinness to my grandmother in memory of her first husband who worked in the engineer's department — Sergeant Daniel Griffith of the 9th Royal Inniskilling Fusiliers, killed in action in 1917. The other side of the family, Ulster Presbyterians, migrated to Wexford and made a name for themselves in commerce there. My father, a Dubliner, often says that the story of the poor Protestant in Dublin has yet to be told.

The complex meandering of my family's Irishness, mirrored in so many other Irish homes, is reinforced. I think again of the futility of the search, so beloved by some, for a pure Irishness, a Celtic Aryanism that, because of our multi-faceted history, is elusive and unobtainable.

Growing up in Cork, in the era of the local shop, culture was branded naïvely as well: Roman Catholic and Protestant. The labels never did justice to the multifarious reality, and the majority seemed to live on the assumption of "sameness". I discovered this at the age of ten in a caravan park in Ownahincha. At the water tap one Sunday morning, an elderly man with a cloth cap sauntered over: "Did you not get Mass yet?" he challenged. Annoyed, I thought, "How dare he assume I'm the same as him." That presumption of sameness was an imposition.

On its part, there were undoubted instances of a smiling sectarianism from within my own community in the 1970s. There was ambivalence about reaching out. We carried social cards signed by our rectors in order to gain admittance to parish dances where we would meet "our own". The need to "stick together" was innate. Many who embarked on their own ecumenical journey in inter-church marriages testify to painful experiences from all sides.

Two formative years at international school in Canada in the late 1970s exploded the pixels of my images of monochrome Ireland. By then Ireland was moving on anyway.

Surprisingly, I've discovered the assumption of "sameness" is still around in 2002. In the spring I brought my children to get their haircuts. "You're in second class," the woman remarks. "You'll be making your First Communion soon." My son blushes and, dislocated ideologically, looks to me for help. I'm wearing my clerical collar. I take the two boys by the hand and we stroll home. Some shoppers have to look twice: the possibility of difference has yet to dawn on them. The collar draws the sneers of some, occasionally articulated.

Much of our administrative infrastructure is predicated still on the assumptions of the prevalent majority religious culture. The proposals in a document about civil registration of marriages produced by the government in 2001, for example, failed to take cognisance of the formalities for marriages within the Church of Ireland as worked since 1844!

A few are more aggressive in their unwillingness to come to terms with the new landscape. Last year at a civic event, mixing with the crowd, I said to a teacher, "I'm Paul Colton, Church of Ireland Bishop of Cork." "There's only one Bishop of Cork," was his retort. Among the exceptional few there is a residual bigotry.

This personal journey as an Irishman makes me what I am and what I say. On Saint Patrick's Day, 2002 I spoke of the need for a new maturity in our definition of Irishness:

> . . . we, in Ireland today, need to come to terms with a fresh and re-evaluated definition of our Irishness — the more so in the light of the arrival here of new and rich cultures. We have to accept that being Irish does not necessarily mean that a person is white, is Roman Catholic, or even Christian, or religious at all, or is married with children, or is heterosexual, or is nationalist or republican, or speaks Irish, or even English.

Rev Patrick Comerford

Rev Patrick Comerford is a priest of the Church of Ireland, the Dublin-based Regional Officer of the Church Missionary Society Ireland and former Foreign Desk Editor of The Irish Times. *In 2001, he co-edited, with Patsy McGarry, the book* Christianity, *based on a series of articles in* The Irish Times *to commemorate the new millennium.*

Céad Míle Fáilte to Repentance and Reconciliation

Sitting on a panel for a Lenten discussion group in Wexford parish in the mid-1990s, I was asked by a concerned parishioner about the plans to mark the bicentenary of the 1798 Rising. She recalled the commemorations in 1948 and 1938, and was worried that 50 or 60 years later, they might once again degenerate into an expression of Catholic triumphalism.

Like many Wexford families, the Comerfords of Bunclody were a mixed bunch: they lie side-by-side with one another in the old graveyard at Kilmyshall and in the churchyard at Saint Colman's in Templeshanbo. In between the rows of graves, it is difficult to tell between those who were buried according to the rites of the Church of Ireland and those buried according to the rites of the Roman Catholic Church. But of one thing we are sure: those who were alive in 1798 had supported the United Irishmen in the Rising.

I have inherited the sword said to have been carried by my grandfather's grandfather, James Comerford, a 23-year-old at the time of the Rising, and buried in Templeshanbo in 1825. And I have inherited some peculiar folk memories from those past generations. One apocryphal story claims that in the days when only officers could afford full uniforms, there was one way in battle to tell soldiers and rebels apart: if a man spoke in English and said his prayers from the *Book of Common Prayer*, he was fighting with the United Irishmen; but if he spoke in Irish and said Catholic prayers he was fighting with the North Cork Militia.

That Lenten evening in Saint Iberius's Church on Wexford's Main Street, I was able to recall a glorious list of Wexford rebels from Church of Ireland families: Beauchamp Bagenal Harvey, Matthew Keugh, and Cornelius Grogan, who were executed on Wexford Bridge in June 1798, as well as Anthony Perry, John Boxwell, William Hughes, William Hatton and George Sparks. And, of course, there was John Kelly, "the Boy from Killanne", who had been churchwarden of St Anne's, Killanne, for most the two decades before the outbreak of the Rising.

The commemorations of 1998 could never have been described as celebrations. Instead, they swept away any fears that there might have been a sectarian "spin" on the events 200 years earlier. There was a moving service at Wexford Bridge to remember all the dead of 1798. There was a public apology from Bishop Brendan Comiskey for sectarian events in the past, including the Fethard-on-Sea boycott. And there was the service on a warm summer's evening in the churchyard at Old Ross, at which we remembered the large numbers put to death in the massacre at Scullabogue Barn, read out their names, and unveiled the first memorial stone ever erected on their mass grave. It was a time for repentance and a time for reconciliation.

If that memorial stone can be attributed to the hard labours and endeavours of any one individual, then that person must be the late Sean Cloney. Sean wanted a memorial that would remember the dead of what is often seen as one of the worst sectarian incidents in Irish history. But, of course, the dead included both Catholics and Protestants, and those engaged in the killings included Protestants as well as Catholics. The names were worth reading aloud, not just to remember the victims and the perpetrators, but because those family names still survive in the surrounding districts and parishes.

We were all guilty together and we were all victims together. But in the intervening generations, our families had refused to talk about those events — the deep divisions, the violence, the sectarianism and the betrayal. But hidden sores fester rather than heal. And so, was it any wonder that, a few short miles from Scullabogue and just a few generations after the burning at the barn, the Fethard-on-Sea boycott came to symbolise the deep, unspoken, yet artificial divide, separating neighbour from neighbour, kinsman from kinsman?

As a child, I grew up in the shadow of the Fethard-on-Sea boycott. It was spoken of in hushed tones throughout the southeast. When I got engaged in Wexford in 1974, it was suggested that, because Barbara was a practising Catholic, we should get married in Dublin: the rules on inter-church marriages were still being interpreted in the strictest and most unkind manner by Bishop Donal Herlihy in the Diocese of Ferns. We got married in Dublin, and settled down to live there. But in the years that followed, Bishop Noel Willoughby and Bishop Brendan Comiskey became pioneers in the ecumenical field as they drew up radical guidelines on the pastoral care of inter-church marriages. If only that prophetic vision and those guidelines had been in place when Sean Cloney and Sheila Kelly got married so many years ago!

Bishop Brendan Comiskey's public apology in Rowe Street Church, Wexford, for the Fethard-on-Sea boycott came during the 1798 commemorations. It was gracious and unequivocal; there were no excuses; there were no qualifications; and it was responded to in the same spirit by Bishop Willoughby's successor, Bishop John Neill. Bagenal Harvey would have been pleased.

A few weeks later, at another 1798 commemoration, during the sort of conversation that takes place after so many such events on this island, I was challenged about John Kelly, the Boy from Killanne, and my assertions about his Protestant identity. I was told, "Kelly is not a Protestant name". I pointed out that there had been Kelly members of the Church of Ireland in the Kilkenny/

Wexford area since at least the late seventeenth century. But I was getting nowhere in my efforts to explore how our identities and family stories are interwoven, how there is no separate Protestant or Catholic identity, how we are all interrelated, until someone who overheard the conversation brought the discussion to a close with a simple statement. "Sure of course John Kelly was a Protestant. What do you think Sheila Cloney's name was before she got married?"

In Old Kilmyshall, one of the burial places for the Comerfords of Bunclody, more of my ancestors rest close to the grave of their cousin Eleanor Kavanagh, Eibhlín A' Rúin, the daughter of Sir Morgan Kavanagh who was the last of his family to live at Clonmullen Castle. Her marriage to William Boote of Enniscorthy, a junior officer in her father's regiment, drove Cearbhall Ó Dálaigh to desperation. On hearing his haunting love song, "Eibhlín A' Rúin", on her wedding day, Eleanor eloped with the harpist. Years later, after Cearbhall's death, Eleanor returned to Clonmullen. When she died at the age of 63 in 1717, she was buried in Old Kilmyshall, close to her cousins and ancestors. One of the best-loved love songs in the collection of great Irish ballads, "Eibhlín A' Rúin" also contains the earliest example in our literature of the use of the term "Céad Míle Fáilte". But it is often forgotten that the song and its beautiful, haunting tune commemorate a woman who was born to one of the great Gaelic Irish families, but who was, nevertheless, a member of the Church of Ireland.

Our families, our stories, our songs and our memories are interwoven: Catholic and Protestant, we are part and parcel of one another, part of one great love story.

Carol Coulter

Carol Coulter was born and grew up in south County Sligo. She attended Alexandra School and College in Dublin, and studied English Language and Literature in Trinity College, Dublin, acquiring both a BA (Mod) and PhD there. She worked as a freelance journalist for a number of years before joining The Irish Times *in 1986. She has a Diploma in Legal Studies and is Legal Affairs Correspondent with* The Irish Times, *and*

is also the author of a number of essays and books on both cultural studies and women's and equality issues. She lives in Dublin with her husband and son.

Shortly after the RTE *States of Fear* series revealed the systematic abuse of children in industrial schools run by religious orders, another smaller, but related, story emerged. This concerned the use of children in a group of Protestant-run orphanages in clinical trials by pharmaceutical companies, without, apparently, the knowledge or consent of the children's families.

The matter received some discussion in the Dáil, and has been referred to the Laffoy Commission on Child Abuse. But what was striking about the story was that, while the backgrounds and situations of the children in the Catholic-run industrial schools received widespread public discussion, no-one thought to inquire about the children in the Protestant orphanages, which continued in existence into the 1970s.

Where did these children come from? Why were they there? Were there really significant numbers of Protestant children unfortunate enough to have lost both parents, and to have no relatives capable of looking after them? If these children did have

living family members, why were they in institutions? None of
these questions were asked, as if they fell outside the known
boundaries of public discourse about Catholic and non-Catholic,
rich and poor, privileged and marginalised, into which the
broader discussion of the Catholic Church and children's institutions fell, and therefore no tools existed for examining them.

I knew a girl who was sent to a Protestant orphanage in the
1960s. She was the daughter of a neighbouring farmer in the west
of Ireland townland where I grew up. All the farms there were
small, and when her father died her mother was unable to support her large family. Some of them were sent to the orphanage in
south County Dublin, where they would receive an elementary
education and eventually, it was assumed, work in the lowest
echelons of the service industry, as domestic servants or, if fortunate, as shop assistants.

I met this girl on a number of occasions while I was at secondary school in Dublin. One of the things that struck me most
sharply on the rare occasions when we were in the city together
was her extreme fear, especially of men. She found it terrifying to
stand at a bus-stop in the company of a man. This fear had been
instilled into her by those running the orphanage, in a crude attempt to prevent their charges from repeating the perceived mistake of many of their mothers — conceiving a child out of
wedlock. Many of the children there had been born to single
mothers, in circumstances where they could not support them.

The misfortune of losing her father deprived this girl of more
than a normal relationship with men — it had deprived her of a
place in the broader, yet close-knit community into which she had
been born. She was now the beneficiary, if such it can be called, of
Protestant charity, and thus trapped in that environment, at the
lowest level of its rigid hierarchy.

In the west of Ireland community where we both grew up, the
handful of Protestant families, most of them small farmers, were
an integral part of the local community, sharing its memory of
evictions and neighbourly solidarity, its customs and superstitions,
its leisure activities, limited as they were to the GAA, dancing,

traditional music and the local pub, along with the occasional escape of its brightest sons and daughters to the cities and the lower
professions via scholarships and the teacher-training colleges.

Such integration was not complete, of course. The ongoing reality of *Ne Temere*, and the influence of Protestant fundamentalism
on the theology of the Church of Ireland, produced a suspicion of
the Catholic Church and a fear of mixed marriages that resulted in
a layer of parallel social activities designed to keep marriages
within the Protestant religious community.

I benefited from the escape route, and in the south Dublin area
where I lived while attending secondary school in the city, I discovered another world, vastly different not only from rural Ireland, but from the Protestant community within it in which I had
grown up. That was the world of the south Dublin Protestant
middle class in the 1960s, a smug and complacent intimate world
where networking assured children employment in the arenas of
finance, insurance and manufacturing, where the old Protestant
middle class still held sway. Its social life was almost hermetically
sealed, with its Scout and Girl Guide troops, its tennis clubs, its
youth clubs, all linked to the Church. Unlike the people I grew up
with, the girls in my school — and, indeed, their parents —
passed their entire lives with practically no social interaction with
their Catholic neighbours.

My first introduction to racism came from this community,
where I overheard comments about both Catholics and Jews that
could only be regarded as racist. This was combined with an An-
glophilia and a snobbishness that I had never encountered before.

Later, when most of my friends were from Catholic backgrounds, I was puzzled and sometimes irritated by the distorted
and extraordinarily benign view they had of the Protestant community in Ireland. The stereotype I encountered then had, like all
stereotypes, little to do with reality. According to the Dublin Catholic middle class from which most of my friends came, Protestants, a
homogenous group, were economically comfortable, diligent, hard-
working, tolerant, and devoted to slightly eccentric though produc-
tive pursuits like market gardening and home-baking.

Such a view does not accommodate differences in historical origin, geography or class. It glosses over the undeniably unpleasant aspects of this history, like the disproportionately powerful grip a section of the Protestant community held, up into the 1960s, on swathes of the Irish economy, and the religious bigotry that was an undercurrent surfacing from time to time. Nor does it accommodate the reality of the economically underprivileged in that community, who were, if anything, even more despised and unrepresented than their Catholic counterparts.

Unlike the latter, their story has never been told. While the orphanages may no longer be open, in both rural and urban Ireland there are still Protestants in the ranks of the working class and small farmers, largely invisible because they do not meet the stereotype held of the community as a whole.

The Protestant community in the Republic of Ireland has, like society as a whole, changed over the past 40 years and, as some of its representatives like the former Archbishop of Dublin, Walton Empey, illustrate, it is a more open and more tolerant community. But it too has its complexities, its internal contradictions and its dark secrets. No discussion of the modernisation of Irish society can afford to trap any part of it in outdated stereotypes.

Edith Newman Devlin

Edith Newman Devlin (nee Gaw) was edu-cated in Dublin at the Diocesan School, Alexandra College and Trinity College. She was awarded an MBE for services to litera-ture (1988) and an honorary D.Litt. from Queen's University, Belfast, also for ser-vices to literature (1993). The author of Speaking Volumes: A Dublin Child-hood *(2000), she is married to Peter (D.D.) Devlin, emeritus professor of English litera-ture at Queen's. They live in Belfast.*

The Poor Protestants of Dublin

In the 1930s and 1940s when I was growing up in Dublin, well-off Protestants were known to live in the better suburbs of Dub-lin — Rathgar, Dalkey, Killiney. They were usually professional people, many with big businesses in town. Not so well known were the poor Protestants who lived in the inner city and shared with their impoverished Catholic neighbours everything except their religion. I knew, for I lived among them. My father, an ex-naval man, was lodge-keeper to the prestigious St Patrick's Private Hos-pital for the Insane (known locally as the madhouse). It stood just off James's Street at the apex of Bow Lane and Steven's Lane and our house was comfortable indeed with parlour, kitchen, scullery, three bedrooms and a garden.

James's Street, Thomas Street, Meath Street, Francis Street and Bow Lane teemed with many poor people, most trying to survive in unhygienic tenements with one family to one or two rooms, no running water and one toilet in the yard for three, four or five families. There was barely enough to eat and TB was widespread. Brawling and drunkenness were everyday occurrences; unemployed men hung around the pubs and betting shops in large inert numbers while poorly clad women tried to raise a few shillings for food at the local pawnshop. Everybody seemed to live "on tick". These were the years of the Great Depression, the Slump, which bore down especially heavily on the Irish poor. A small minority of Protestants lived alongside our Catholic neighbours, sharing their conditions but going to a separate school and a separate church. Our school, the Church of Ireland National School, St James's was further down the street nearly opposite the Catholic chapel. There were many poor Protestants in our school, some with no shoes, even in winter (Mrs Kelly, the Master's wife, often bought shoes and clothes for these pupils out of her own pocket); lips were blue with cold and trousers as likely to be attached with a rusty nail as with a button. The poorest lived in the worst accommodation of all, in Nash's Court and Lamb's Court off James's Street, which were so rough that we were afraid to go into them. Two pupils lived in a caravan on waste ground on the way to Kilmainham. Opposite our school was the dreaded workhouse or Dublin Union, the bitterest and last humiliation of the destitute. There must have been Protestants among them.

My best friend was a Catholic from Bow Lane. Two rooms had to accommodate parents, a bed-ridden grandmother and three children. There was no running water and only one toilet in the yard for four families. The grunting of pigs could be heard in the makeshift sheds of the owner nearby. Martha and I roamed the streets at will and knew every house, every shop, every grating intimately. With her I learned Catholic ways and how to pass myself off as a Catholic when it made me more comfortable to do so. At that time the Catholic Church had a very public presence and you could not pass along a single street without being aware of it. We went to our church service on Sundays only but the Catholic churches stood open all day and at all hours with people continually streaming in and out to attend mass or just to say a prayer. Through the open door, we would catch a glimpse of huge waxen statues hanging on the cross, Sacred Hearts dripping with gouts of blood, candles blazing and rows of women with heads bent in

devotion and countless rosaries passing patiently through innumerable fingers. All these were "idols" to us Protestants. We
stared at them in bewildered incomprehension. When passing a
chapel, on foot or by tram, men doffed their caps and everyone
made the sign of the cross. We Protestants did nothing and felt
strangely awkward. Three times a day, the Angelus rang out over
Dublin and everyone blessed themselves and said a "Hail Mary".
She did not figure in our observances.

Catholics expressed their religious feeling openly and continually. They invoked the name of God, His Son, His Holy
Mother and all the Saints with dramatic emphasis — "Jesus, Mary
and Joseph!" was the overture to dramatic statements of all sorts.
This for us was to break the Commandment "Thou shalt not take
the name of the Lord in vain". It was blasphemy and we were
simply unable to do it. We kept our spiritual feelings (if we had
them) strictly to ourselves. It would have been unthinkable for a
Protestant clergyman, breviary in hand, to say his prayers on the
street as priests did. And there seemed to be many priests on
Dublin's streets in blacker-than-black clerical outfits, remote pres-
ences, inscrutable expressions on their faces. I learned to say, after
Martha, "God bless you father" to which the priest returned "God
bless you child". They were treated with the utmost reverence,
unlike the nuns with exotic headdresses, long flowing garments
and crucifixes hanging from their waists, who disappeared regularly into the many bleak convents.

Our worship took place on Sunday mornings preceded by
Sunday school, where we were taught the stories of the Bible and,
for doctrine, the Catechism. We learned that we were Protestants
but Catholics too — very confusing — not Roman Catholics, we
must never forget that, but Catholics all the same. Somewhere in
the remote past an event called the Reformation had taken place
after the Catholic Church had taken a wrong turning. It wor-
shiped idols and other wrong things but we had cleansed it of
those practices and had gone on to be the True Church, reformed
and strengthened. We felt neither reformed nor strengthened. We
were just "different". Catholic blood seemed to flow in every vein

but ours. This was unsettling at a deeply unconscious level to a child who wanted to be like everyone else and to sink anonymously into a known and familiar background. For all that, there was no hostility or aggressiveness shown towards us by our Catholic neighbours. They were openly kind and affectionate and in their poverty never stopped thanking God for his mercies. Many a time in a poor Catholic house, I was wrapped around with warmth I did not get at home. There was also a certain respect for their Protestant neighbours — "all those lovely Protestants going to their church to the tolling of the bell" said Martha's kindly mother. It was just a pity that they were forever condemned to remain outside the One True Church.

Later, as a pupil at the Church of Ireland secondary school in Adelaide Road, there was a great emphasis on all things Irish. We spent many hours learning the language, we competed in Irish dancing competitions in the Mansion House, we went to the occasional church services in Irish.

Bean Uí de Valera, the great man's wife, came to give out the prizes at our school. In spite of this, we knew in a vague sort of way that we were not considered "the real thing", for we were Protestants and must only be playing at being Irish. Real Irish enthusiasts wore *fáinnes* in their lapels and some were doing all their schoolwork through "the medium" as a sign of their dedication to the national culture.

The Protestant–Catholic divide impinged on me more personally when my sister and two brothers married Catholics. The *Ne Temere* decree was in full force and mixed marriages were frowned upon. My sister was married in a Catholic church but at the steps of the sanctuary only. There was no blessing and the parish priest refused to attend the reception afterwards. Thus was the frozen face of the Catholic Church turned to such marriages. When children were born, I was not asked to their baptism or first communion or any of the great religious events in their lives. A mental barrier was erected which separated those who naturally belonged together. The version of Christianity in which I had been brought up was, it seemed, tainted and unacceptable. I wish it had been otherwise.

Roger Downer

Professor Roger G.H. Downer was born in Belfast and educated at the Methodist College and Queen's University Belfast (BSc 1964, MSc 1967). He emigrated to Canada in 1967, obtained his PhD from the University of Western Ontario in 1970 and embarked on an academic career at the University of Waterloo (1970–96) where he served at various times as Professor and Chair of Biology and Vice-President. He spent sabbatical leaves at Hokkaido University, Japan and Oxford University. In 1996,  *he was appointed President of the Asian Institute of Technology in Bangkok and since 1998 has served as President of the University of Limerick. He is author or co-author of 164 research papers in biological chemistry and editor or co-editor of four books. He is a Fellow of the Royal Society of Canada, holder of the Fry Gold Medal and the ESC Gold Medal; Chair of Birr Scientific and Heritage Foundation; Chair of the National Self-Portrait Collection; Vice-Chair, National Technology Park; Vice-Chair, Hunt Museum; Director, Shannon Development; Director, Irish Peace Institute. He is married to Jean and has three children, Kevin, Kathleen and Tara.*

Ireland and the Integration of Religious Minorities: A Personal Perspective

It is not difficult to assume minority status. As a bespectacled child in Belfast, I was subjected to cries of "specky four eyes" by my 20/20 contemporaries. As a newly arrived immigrant in Canada, not versed in the lore of ice hockey and baseball, I was excluded from much of the casual small talk that is part of everyday social interaction. As a westerner living in Asia, I endured the stares, whispers and occasional giggles that accompanied any foray into a public place. Yet in none of these situations did I feel threatened, disadvantaged or discriminated against in any way. Instinctively, I understood the need for children to establish pecking order and I was equally assertive in taunting peers whom I considered to be of lesser athletic or intellectual prowess than me. My Canadian friends soon taught me about their history and culture whereas the curiosity of the Asians was flattering and resulted in many fascinating conversations and insights about a culture that is very different to mine.

These experiences have helped to shape a personal philosophy which rejects any temptation to bear the yoke of perceived persecution and may have contributed to the ease with which my wife and I have adjusted to the situation of living as Protestants in the Republic of Ireland. However, such a rationale is inappropriate and arrogant because I feel that the transition would have been easy irrespective of previous experience. Since our arrival in Limerick four years ago, we have been welcomed by the various communities with which we interact. We work, socialise and worship with Catholics and Protestants and feel a deeper sense of Christian, as opposed to religious commitment here than in any other place where we have lived. We are fully integrated into the local community and have enjoyed the type of welcoming acceptance that would be expected in any society with a strong Christian ethos.

It is sobering to consider if our recent experience would have been similar if, as Catholics, we had moved into a Protestant-dominated district of Northern Ireland. Regrettably, I doubt that it would have been so.

The concluding chapter of Marianne Elliott's excellent history, *The Catholics of Ulster*, is titled "A Resentful Belonging". It is a sad statement on the fate of the 430,000 Catholics and their descendents who were separated politically from their national roots and much of their cultural heritage by the Government of Ireland Act of 1920. The resentment of the Catholic community reflects the failure of successive Unionist governments to integrate these citizens into the newly formed country. The tragic consequences of these failures have plagued the social and economic development of Northern Ireland, deprived the country from availing fully of the creative and intellectual talent of a sizeable percentage of the population and resulted in the horrible violence of the last 35 years.

By contrast, the 90,000 Protestants who became part of the Irish Free State at the time of partition were integrated much more successfully into the new nation. In spite of some instances of blatant discrimination, the Protestant minority demonstrates considerable pride, passion and loyalty for the Republic of Ireland and has been afforded opportunity to contribute to the advancement of the State, with two Protestants elected to the highest office of President of Ireland.

A variety of explanations can be advanced to account for the differing responses of two groups of people on the same small island to the challenges of religious integration. Perhaps the most obvious relates to the relative size of the two minorities. The Catholics in the North were perceived as a serious threat to the power base of the Protestant majority. This led to the introduction of discriminatory measures which suppressed the opportunities available to Catholics and fuelled the fires of Catholic resentment. Fear of the emergence of a Catholic ascendancy also prevented the Protestant political leadership from introducing the types of policies that are essential for full integration of any minority group. The situation in the south was much more favourably disposed towards integration, with Eamon de Valera and other political leaders actively condemning religious discrimination in any form.

Cultural and educational factors contributed also to the different abilities of the two religious minorities to integrate. The fundamental tenet of unionism is retention of British sovereignty and, as a child educated in a Protestant school in Belfast, I was taught British history, British achievements and instilled with a sense of loyalty and respect for the Union flag and the British royal family. My Catholic counterparts in separate, segregated Catholic schools were taught much more Irish history, learned Irish language and developed a love of Ireland and its rich cultural heritage. Thus, there was considerable dichotomy in the background and perspective of the two communities. This contrasted with the situation in the Republic of Ireland, where Catholic and Protestant children followed a common curriculum which encouraged an awareness of and pride in the nation and its traditions.

In addition to the political, educational and cultural factors which militated against successful integration of the Catholic minority in Northern Ireland, differences in the underlying dogma of Protestantism and Catholicism must also be considered. The essence of the Protestant tradition is the freedom and responsibility of an individual to develop a relationship with God that is shaped by personal lived experience. Thus, individual belief, while founded in the central doctrine of Christianity, will reflect an ever-changing human condition. It is this freedom that has resulted in the evolution of many different Protestant denominations. The flexibility afforded by this freedom also makes it easier for a Protestant minority to adapt and live compatibly in a Catholic-dominated society. Catholicism, on the other hand, respects the ultimate authority and hierarchy of the Church as the mystical body of Christ, is obedient to the dictates of the Church and its followers will have greater difficulty in adapting to a society which does not embrace or accept fully the Catholic tradition.

It has been argued that it is nationalism which creates nations rather than the reverse and Ireland provides an example of how, on this small Island, two forms of "nationalism" based on religious beliefs have led to the creation of two nations. A worthy goal of any two adjoining nations is harmonious coexistence and in order for this to occur, there must be mutual respect for and tolerance of the beliefs, traditions and "nationalism" of the other. My experience as a Protestant living in the Republic of Ireland suggests that in this nation such tolerance exists. My wish is that other Protestants from Northern Ireland will have the opportunity to share the positive experience enjoyed by my wife and me.

Rev John Faris

John Faris's grandfather came from Cork, where his father, originally from County Leitrim, ran a wholesale tea-blending business in Washington Street. John was born in Belfast in 1952 and took degrees in classics and divinity in England and Scotland, before training as a Presbyterian minister. He served in a group of congregations in County Fermanagh before becoming minister of the Presbyterian churches in Aghada and Cork in 1988. He also serves as Clerk of the Presbytery of Dublin & Munster which covers congregations in Connacht, Leinster and Munster. He is married to Heather and they have two children, Naomi and Peter. Although the whole family was born in Ulster, they now support Munster's rugby team.

My first hospital visit in Cork in August 1988 was in the early evening; a prayer service from the hospital chapel was relayed into the ward. As the rosary echoed around us, the patient I was visiting expressed his annoyance and explained to me that was one of the things you just put up with. I observed that not one person in the ward was paying any attention to the broadcast. They went on reading the paper or playing cards. It was a little picture of a religious society in transition. If the relays still happen, they are unlikely to attract greater devotion 14 years later in an increasingly secular culture.

In March 2002, David Trimble's remarks that the Republic of Ireland was a monocultural sectarian State ruffled feathers. My reaction as a Presbyterian minister living in the Republic of Ireland is that it is actually a society becoming progressively less monocultural, but the uneasy reception of asylum-seekers is one indicator that that we have a lot to do to justify the claim of being a tolerant pluralist society. I sense residual sectarianism in the Republic, with insufficient "closure" on the sectarian violence connected with the foundations of this State. The commemoration of Kevin Barry and the others given State funerals in the autumn of 2001 upset me. I felt it needed to be balanced by an acknowledgement of the human pain and loss of others who suffered in the same conflicts. Not long after Trimble's remarks I heard the view "let the British leave and let them fight it out up there" actually expressed in a discussion about peace at an ecumenical service. I found that deeply hurtful as one reared in a Protestant tradition in the North who has sought to identify as Irish and who wants to see a peaceful reconciliation of the nationalist and unionist aspirations. I don't believe that anyone desiring peace can simply dismiss or ignore those in the North who in good conscience find their identity closer to Scotland and to Britain.

When we moved to Cork from County Fermanagh it was not fully a year after the Enniskillen bomb tragedy, which touched our lives significantly. One thing that struck me was the comparative lack of interest in that event. Someone advised me that, whereas Limerick for example was moved by the tragedy, there was a lesser response in Cork, for whatever reason. We began to get the impression that even for Cork Protestants the North was a faraway place, best not talked about or thought about.

Of course, there was a steep learning curve in changing our attitudes and assumptions to adapt to a culture where Presbyterians were a minority among the Protestant minority and where most Cork people know nothing about us, or the only thing they have heard (inaccurately) is that Ian Paisley is a Presbyterian. Apart from one or two crank phone calls, I have never encountered overtly anti-Protestant attitudes, but I soon noted that some of our older members, while protesting that they got on very well with their Catholic neighbours, could also talk quietly about traumatic events in their childhoods or in the experience of their parents and neighbours. I began to sense a repressed sectarianism among both Protestants and Catholics, a craving for good ecumenical relationships at all costs and a fear of conscientiously expressed difference.

This was crystallised for me in a sad episode in 1990. I had taken the view that I would attend ecumenical prayer services but that, apart from funerals and marriages, I would decline invitations to what were often engagingly called "ecumenical masses". I felt and still feel that the Mass is an exclusively Roman Catholic ceremony; it was not simply that non-Catholics may not receive communion (as *One Bread* has since restated) but that there are profound differences in the Reformed as compared to the Roman Catholic approach to how the death of Christ is represented in the sacrament. There came an invitation to an "ecumenical mass" in Cork City Hall to commemorate the fiftieth anniversary of the "Emergency" first declared in 1940. I sent a polite refusal, while sending greetings, affirming the significance of the anniversary and stating that some of our members had served the State during the "Emergency" in the armed and civic services. I do not know how this was received by the organisers, but one of my members who had served in the "Emergency" took grave exception to my absence. It became clear in discussion with him and others that my refusal to participate in such events was regarded as negative, bigoted and offensive. It was felt to be discourteous to refuse invitations, regardless of one's personal convictions about the nature of the event.

This conflict with fellow Presbyterians was never fully resolved to everyone's satisfaction. I noticed, however, in the 1990s that there were fewer invitations to "ecumenical masses". Was this an indication of a more secular trend, or communication of the official policy of the Diocese of Cork and Ross that the Mass was not appropriate in an ecumenical setting? Paradoxically, in the new century the issue of concern ecumenically is how far there may be "inter-faith" rather than "inter-church" services. The issue has become not the celebration of the Mass but whether or not the name of Christ may be used or the Trinity affirmed. I notice how Presbyterians and Roman Catholics, for all our differences, can often arrive at the same conclusions working from conservative dogmatic bases, in contrast to liberal Protestants. (*Dominus Iesus*, therefore, was not a total turn-off for many Presbyterians.)

One lesson I draw from these impressions is that the formal public ecumenical (and/or inter-faith) service has many difficulties. It often serves as window dressing, repressing many sincerely held differences. Instead, we need to talk and to talk honestly and seek to deal with our differences, our anxieties and our resentments.

Desmond FitzGerald
The Knight of Glin

The Honourable Desmond FitzGerald is the 29th Knight of Glin. His home is the magnificent Glin Castle on the Shannon Estuary. To see and hear the Knight describe a piece of furniture is a history lesson in itself, replete with facts, figures and sometimes folktales. He stands a pace back, his left hand placed under his chin, surveys the subject and, without pause, utters forth perhaps the most comprehensive, analytical and informative description of the artefact that you are likely to hear anywhere.

The Knights of Glin are a branch of the great Norman family, the FitzGeralds or Geraldines, Earls of Desmond, who were granted extensive lands in the early fourteenth century by their Desmond overlords. Three of the cadet branches of the Desmond family were known as the White Knight, the Knight of Glin and the Knight of Kerry. The last White Knight died in 1611 and the title is now extinct. The Knight of Kerry now lives in England. The Glin FitzGeralds survived the Elizabethan, Cromwellian and Jacobite wars, where they were invariably on the losing side, fighting against the English with their kinsmen the Earls of Desmond.

I am the latest in the long line of FitzGeralds to live in and take care of Glin Castle, along with my wife Olda. The castle started as a seventeenth-century thatched house, was expanded in the 1730s, and first acquired grandeur later in the eighteenth century. Glin today is definitely not just a museum, with its paintings, family portraits, Irish furniture and decoration — it is very much a living entity. It is still being adapted and expanded to meet the needs of the different generations of my family who live here or visit. The house is run as a stately bed, breakfast and dinner establishment and is an ideal place to entertain guests and carry on the tradition of hospitality for which it was originally built. This expansion of the activities in the house demonstrates the adaptation to the modern world that is so necessary to the economic sustainability of the place.

I feel totally Irish, not that I think anything of nationalism — it has caused — is causing — so much grief in the world. Am I accepted here? I feel part of Ireland but I'm not sure that Ireland knows what to do with me and my tribe. As well as having served on numerous committees concerned with heritage issues, I have been a member of the Irish Georgian Society since the 1960s and its President for nine years. I find it interesting that I've never been invited to a State function. Not one dinner in Dublin Castle in all those years! However, I was recently conferred with an honorary doctorate of letters by Trinity College Dublin and I am in favour of some sort of an honours system that acknowledges the efforts of people who work for the common good. State boards, even the National Gallery, are dominated by political appointees to the extent that there is often little room for culture. The fact is that these boards are often used as an alternative honours system but so many people who do make a contribution remain unsung, which seems to me to be a pity. As for me, I get on with taking care of the house and with my writing on art and the history of art. *Ireland's Paintings*, my most important book, was written in collaboration with Professor Anne Cruickshank and published in late 2002. Through all of this, I stay deeply attached to Ireland and remain attached to educational concerns involved in Irish art and architecture.

The "old decency" was favoured in the early days, post the 1922 difficulties, but I'm not sure that anyone values our culture these days. In effect, we were emasculated from political life and left to vegetate in the few remaining beautiful houses of Ireland that were still in private hands. Admittedly, Henry Mountcharles did make an effort to break into politics but he is a noble exception and greatly to be praised for restoring Slane Castle after that devastating fire. I never had any time for the "true Gael" pretentious nonsense. I think it was beneficial that young people were forced to emigrate, learnt so much and then, in many cases, came back to challenge our little-Irish nationalism.

The Protestants did a lot for this country but we are just as much to blame as anyone in our attitude to the conservation of Ireland's religious architectural heritage. So I can share the concerns of many at what Bishop Casey did to the beautiful Pugin cathedral in Killarney.

I acknowledge gratefully the government tax breaks that facilitate the restoration of houses like Glin. I have to say, however, that I know very few politicians personally — a failure on my behalf. In my experience, politicians generally don't seem to be interested in taking care of our heritage. However, my neighbour and Fine Gael TD Jimmy Deenihan is a noble exception and I just wish that more of his peers would engage with heritage matters. The fact that the whole planning issue in Ireland is in such turmoil is a source of great concern and I worry if society cares enough to see that matters are put to right.

As one of the last survivors of the old landowning caste in Ireland, I see my stewardship of the house, and of Georgian Ireland, as a voyage of discovery. The place never lets me or my wife and three daughters rest. We welcome people to stay most of the year, so the house and the estate is more full of people than for many years. This enables us to keep going financially, but does not guarantee the future. We live with the spectre of the auctioneer's tent going up in the garden and seeing everything scattered in a couple of days.

In conversation with Colin Murphy

Rosemary French

Rosemary French is a member of the Church of Ireland. She was Chairman of the Board of the Adelaide Hospital/Adelaide Hospital Society from 1995–98, and of the Adelaide and Meath Hospital, Dublin, incorporating the National Children's Hospital, from 1996–99.

I was brought up in a Church of Ireland parish in south County Dublin in the 1950s and 1960s. My school, Park House in Donnybrook, was an unusual one, run on independent inter-denominational lines. My social life as a teenager was in a pro-tected environment — parish dances, Girl Guides, hockey club and mixing with the children of my parents' friends. I married my husband, Ian, also a member of the Church of Ireland, in 1968, and we have two daughters. I am now a triple granny! Growing up, it never struck me that I was any different from the majority of citizens in the Republic of Ireland. However, it is now clear to me that I was unaware of the general state of things at the time. My parents had made sacrifices so that we would have a choice in terms of private education and private medicine. The State did not provide for our needs according to our beliefs.

During the early 1970s, it began to dawn on me that perhaps it was a bit different for us. My circle of friends widened through my interests and through my children. Issues such as family plan-ning, wider health issues, education being controlled by the ma-jority denomination, began to be discussed at national level. Choices did not exist where I had innocently presumed they did.

In the mid-1980s, I was invited to join the Board of the Adelaide Hospital, then in Peter Street, Dublin. There I found a group of people who were committed to the voluntary support of a public hospital, which had been serving people of all denominations since 1835. I discovered that all was far from equal in the provision of healthcare in our State. Most did not have the choice. When patients turned up at most hospitals they had to accept the treatment according to the ethos of the Roman Catholic Church. Absolutely nothing wrong with this if it fitted in with your beliefs, but clearly everyone did not share in such beliefs. In the Adelaide Hospital, patient confidentiality was protected under its governing Charter.

During the 1980s, with the closure of Dr Steeven's Hospital, Baggot Street Hospital, Mercers Hospital, all in Dublin, and then Barringtons Hospital in Limerick, the last hospital left in the State with an ethos which was not that of the Roman Catholic Church was the Adelaide Hospital. It was being starved of funds and it looked as if it was being squeezed out of existence. The Board of the hospital had to fight publicly and very bravely for the hospital's survival. The Board agreed to commence negotiations to become part of the new hospital due to be built in Tallaght. These negotiations were long and protracted, and I remain puzzled as to why it should have been so difficult to get agreement for one hospital in the State to have a multi-denominational and pluralist character. It was a lonely place to be but one could feel the winds of change blowing in the country and the Board of the Adelaide Hospital received incredible support from people of all denominations and of none throughout the whole country.

In 1995, I was elected Chairman of the Adelaide Hospital, After more protracted negotiations with the Department of Health, the Government and our sister hospitals, the National Children's Hospital and the Meath Hospital, it was agreed that an amended Adelaide Hospital Charter would be used as the governing instrument for the new hospital and that these three hospitals would amalgamate and move to Tallaght as soon as possible. In 1996, the Charter was amended in the Dáil and the hospitals moved to Tallaght in June 1998. It was a great feeling to be part of an exciting development in our country enshrined by an Act of the Oireachtas. The Board of the hospital now had, by law, the responsibility to maintain the hospital as a focus for Protestant participation in the health services and to preserve its particular denominational ethos, while at the same time maintaining the freedom of conscience and the free profession and practice of religion by all within the hospital. It is in the achieving of such a fine balance that the true character of the hospital can be demonstrated. The Protestant community, together with other minority religions under the Charter, had now been given an identifiable role to play in the provision of healthcare in our country.

But there were dark clouds on the horizon. The hospital in its infancy had to survive a financial crisis, and as a result lost its chief executive officer who had come from Canada, bringing with him many new and enlightened ways of delivering healthcare, but it did survive and now is heading into a challenging and formative time in its history. The hospital staff and those who are part of its governing structure face the responsibility and challenge of developing an institution which will play its part as an independent voluntary teaching hospital in a modern pluralist society. Hopefully it can be a beacon of light in the whole island of Ireland, demonstrating that we can share and participate in the care of all in a very clear, respectful and practical way.

On a personal note, I admit that during some turbulent times, as a Protestant I felt different, unwelcome and at times frightened. But I was sustained by the example and support of others in roles of leadership who desired change and freedom from the constraints of the "one way" of doing things. Change is happening very rapidly and hopefully we can all play our part in a real way in creating a society where difference is openly cherished. This can only become a reality through open and fair availability of services so that each citizen has the freedom to choose, regardless of geographical location or financial means. I fear we have some way to go. Perhaps there lies the challenge for all of us.

Rev Ferran Glenfield

Ferran Glenfield is rector of Kill O'The Grange Parish, Blackrock, County Dublin, and is a graduate of Trinity College, Dublin and Oxford. He is married to Jean and has three children.

Time is full of potential. The Old Testament preacher, Qoheleth, captured this in the immortal lines of the third chapter of Ecclesiastes: "For everything there is a season and a time for every matter under heaven." What is the time for Protestantism in the Irish Republic? At the start of the new millennium, an unlikely source claimed that a "Protestant Movement" now exists in the Republic. David Quinn, editor of the *Irish Catholic*, suggested that the decline of the Catholic Church has created a gap in the religious landscape. Ironically, Quinn saw a renaissance of Ulster Scots Presbyterianism, rather than the Church of Ireland, filling the gap.

In normal Irish usage, the term Protestant was used in a limited sense and meant being a member of the Church of Ireland. Although by far the largest Protestant denomination in the Republic, the Church of Ireland is uneasy about its Protestant credentials. What are the reasons for this? One reason is the association of Protestantism with extremism, notably in Northern Ireland. From a southern Protestant perspective, Ulster Protestantism is regarded as sectarian, divisive and intolerant. The silhouetted spire of Drumcree Church has become a visible symbol of extremism, an albatross over Protestantism.

A second reason for the Protestant character of the Church of Ireland is that of negation, whereby Protestant identity is defined by what it is not, rather than what it is. Definition by negation is seen in terms of reaction and a distancing from, as opposed to a confident affirmation of Protestant principles. Such a disposition does not sit easily with the times. Thirdly, in an ecumenical era, the Church of Ireland has sought to distance itself from its Reformation roots. Indeed there are those within the Church who see the Reformation as possibly the greatest tragedy to befall Western Christianity. Thus the Reformation principles of the Church of Ireland enunciated in the Thirty-Nine Articles of Religion and affirmed in the Preamble and Declaration, adopted by the General Convention in 1870, are merely assumed rather than engaged.

Since the 1960s, the Protestant identity of the Church of Ireland in the Republic has given way to the ethos of Anglicanism. Synthesis as opposed to antithesis has been promoted, Protestant propositions replaced by emphasis on sacred space, symbol, liturgy and priesthood. Prominence is placed on balance and moderation instead of theology and practice. In a sense, the Church of Ireland in the Republic has become progressively a form of liberal Catholicism. Increasingly, Church of Ireland clergy look and behave like Catholic priests in the act of worship itself.

Not surprisingly, the excising of the Protestant character of the Church of Ireland in the Republic has confused and demoralised its lay members. Moreover, it has largely failed to compensate for dwindling ranks by attracting sufficient numbers of lapsed Catholics. Of course, the decline of the Church of Ireland in southern Ireland has been long and steady. It would appear that the decline is entering a terminal phase as the Church enters the third Christian millennium.

Declan Kiberd, Professor of Anglo-Irish literature in UCD, has noted that just before a culture goes under, it often achieves a grace of lyric utterance, a swan song. Such vocalisation encapsulates all the values, aspirations and achievements of the culture, before it finally lies down and dies. Perhaps the steady stream of memoirs and reflections from southern Protestant writers in recent times is an expression of the legendary song. As with the demise of the Anglo-Irish and the death of southern unionism, the Church of Ireland faces its swan song.

However, the history of Ireland is replete with great reversals. There may well be a time for the Church of Ireland to rediscover its Protestant identity and to make headway. There is much to commend it to the Irish people. Its appeal to antiquity beyond the Reformation to the Celtic Church and ultimately to the early Church of the Acts of the Apostles is very real. The Church of Ireland is no recent "blow-in": it is part of the otherness of Ireland.

That quaintly named body "the Board of First Fruits" saw to it that plentiful Protestant churches were woven into the Irish landscape. Many still exist and are the focus of small worshipping communities, often with a hinterland of estranged Protestants. Enough time has lapsed to dispel the old chestnut that the Church of Ireland is an English religious garrison. It is a distinctly Irish church, whose historical baggage seems light by comparison to the crushing weight upon the contemporary Catholic Church.

Nonetheless, if the Church of Ireland is to recapture the religious imagination of Irish people, there is remedial work to be done. This will involve a recall to its calling as an agent of the Gospel, with confidence in the truth, relevance and power in the apostolic Gospel received in the New Testament. A Church which exists for and is focused on the uniqueness and finality of Jesus Christ and invites people to a personal experience of Him. A Church where faith and learning is developed by rigorously reflecting on the content of faith, thus re-endowing it with weight and substance. A Church where there is a profound sense of belonging and yet with an open and generous disposition to a secular Ireland. One whose members live out an authentic Christian lifestyle, distinct but appealing, where the worship of the Church, the interior life, is mirrored by an exterior life of witness and social action. A Church which has critical connection with evolving Irish cultures and which seeks to transform them.

As it stands, the Church of Ireland is too feeble to attract the spiritually needy and too superficial to attract the seriously thoughtful. The spiritually needy will gravitate to newer Churches, the thoughtful will find their home in Presbyterianism or other spiritual islands in the sea of secularism. Before the swan song swells, regret lingers, expressed in Patrick Kavanagh's "Raglan Road": "the sun shines down on Grafton Street and we not making hay".

Dean Victor Griffin

A native of County Wicklow, the Very Reverend Victor Griffin was installed as Dean of St Patrick's Cathedral in 1969, having served for 22 years in parishes in Northern Ireland, in the city of Derry. Thus a ministry of 44 years was divided equally between Northern Ireland and the Republic, a unique experience. He retired in 1991 and now lives in Limavady.

I can still hear ringing in my ears my mother's warning, "Victor, keep off religion and politics or you'll get us all burnt out." Protestants who remained after 1922 understandably kept a low profile. Associated in the public mind with the old enemy, the British ascendancy, they had "to watch their step". In the new Irish Free State where Irishness was generally seen as synonymous with being Roman Catholic, anti-British, nationalist and lover of all things Gaelic, Protestants felt less than the genuine article. The tacit acceptance of a Catholic State for a Catholic people was made painfully obvious by successive governments sending messages of allegiance and filial loyalty to the Pope. Segregation was the rule in schools and churches.

Ecumenism and pluralism were unknown. Each denomination was convinced that it had the truth, the whole truth and nothing but the truth. When challenged as to what denomination Jesus would prefer were he to return, the inevitable reply by priest or minister was, "I don't think he'd wish to change."

After national school in Carnew, County Wicklow, I was sent to Kilkenny College, an austere Protestant boarding school. Arrayed on Sundays in Eton suits and mortar boards, we were figures of fun, or at the very least objects of curiosity to the local populace. "Proddy Woddy cups and saucers", jeered some. Not only did we attend a Protestant school, but we wore the badge of our peculiar separateness. Playing or watching games of any sort on Sundays was out of the question, a flagrant breach of "the Sabbath", and the decision to allow boys to play tennis on Sunday afternoons caused uproar among some parents. The GAA, with its ban on "foreign games" and its association with anti-British republicanism, held no appeal for Protestants. Four years later in 1940, passing Croke Park on my way from Mountjoy School, then in Mountjoy Square, to our sports field in Clontarf, little did I imagine that I would be the first Protestant clergyman to make my way to a GAA final there, and on a Sunday too (for things were beginning to change in the 1970s).

After austere Kilkenny College and relaxed Mountjoy School, came Trinity in 1942, then very much a Protestant, indeed unionist, university, since large numbers of students from the Protestant and unionist tradition came from Northern Ireland, including Presbyterian divinity students from Magee College, Derry, who took Trinity degrees. Unionist students on the College roof gave full vent to their loyalty to the crown on VE Day, which resulted in the burning of the Union flag by republicans in College Green, followed by the burning of the Irish Tricolour by the students, my first direct experience of unionist/republican conflict. The story is told that a Northern Ireland Protestant nationalist student, that rare specimen, had his outside windows stoned by republicans and his inside ones by unionists!

My father, a man of many parts — farmer, shopkeeper, motor engineer and funeral undertaker, who brought the first wireless set to Carnew — was a risk-taker, incurably reckless, never interested in making money, widely known for his generosity to all and sundry. Although a devout member of the Church of Ireland, religious denomination was always secondary to him, for all were children of the one God and Father. When the Angelus rang, he would say to his Roman Catholic helpers, "Now you say your prayers and I'll say mine."

My mother came from a family of small farmers in County Monaghan. She had a flair for fashion and after some time as a milliner in Clones, moved south to Carnew to become a millinery buyer in a department store. She was practical and frugal, a necessary foil to an audacious and unpredictable husband, in complete and competent control of the domestic and financial front. I have a sheaf of unpaid bills in her neat handwriting — it was she who kept the accounts — held together by a long-since rusted safety pin, itemising the account to the Carnew IRA in October 1922 for the hire of cars, many of them having come back to the garage the worse for wear during the Civil War.

While segregation, "them and us", was the rule in schools (except for rugby, which Protestants and Roman Catholic secondary schools played) and churches, thankfully it never obtained in the local farming and business community. Protestants and Roman Catholics intermingled, would drop into each others' homes for an evening fireside chat, when the talk usually centred on the price of cattle, the state of the crops, recent marriages and deaths. The only hint of embarrassment came when there was a mixed marriage. Both sides remained silent. I suppose by a sort of tolerant tacit mutual agreement, mention of such matters was ruled out. The unjust *Ne Temere* decree meant that all the children had to be brought up as Roman Catholics causing a marked decline in the Protestant population and much resentment of the Roman Catholic Church.

Courtown Harbour was our Mecca during the summer holidays. On Sundays and Church feast days, such as the 29th of June and 15th of August, swimmers and splashers, farmers and their families made this pilgrimage, many on the off-chance of meeting some friends, distant cousins or old acquaintances. Weather-beaten sons of the soil, Protestant and Catholic, dressed in Sunday best would sit together on the wall gazing out to sea, discussing the price of land or the state of the crops. Then, at the approach of darkness, all were homeward bound, except the cinema-goers and dance-hallers. But for the Protestants, there was no cinema or dance-hall. Such breaking of the Sabbath was frowned on and any infringement was seen as a lukewarm attitude to the faith and the first step on the road to a mixed marriage and the dreaded consequence of capitulation to Rome.

From 1947 to 1969, I ministered in Derry where the accolade "Griffin the Fenian" was bestowed on me by fanatical Protestant unionists who were enraged by my criticism of Stormont and the neglect of the north-west. Then in 1969, I came to Dublin where my advocacy of a more tolerant pluralist society free from Church domination was greeted with "Griffin, another Paisley" by a TD in the Dáil. Now all is changing. The unholy mixture of Irish identity and politics, both North and south, is losing its potency, except among the Northern diehards. When Irishness is seen as transcending religion and politics, more a sense of place, of belonging, of being at home in a common homeland, then all can rejoice in the victory of inclusiveness over exclusiveness, of a common unity not limited but enhanced by diversity.

Senator Mary Henry

Senator Mary Henry was elected to Seanad Eireann in 1993 and re-elected in 1997, as an independent, to represent Dublin University. She is married to John McEntagart and has three children. She graduated from Trinity College with a BA in English and an MB in medicine, proceeding to take her MD in 1968. She is deeply committed to improving health care, especially for women, and to encouraging women doctors to continue their professional careers. She was conferred with an Honorary Doctorate of Science by the University of Ulster in 1999 for her work in encouraging women to become involved in public and political life. She feels that civic society in Northern Ireland has, to a great extent, been held together by women.

St Michael's Church of Ireland parish in Blackrock, Cork, was thriving when I was a child in the 1940s and 1950s. There was a two-teacher school and the church was full on Sundays. Admittedly, the attendees at church came from several miles around but one certainly had no feeling of isolation or being excluded from life in the area.

When a parish council was set up in Blackrock village, my father was asked to sit on it. Whether he was the token Protestant or not I don't know, but I believe the only decision he had to make with any denominational connotations was the naming of a newly built council park, "Marian Park", in honour of the Marian Year. I think my father was more concerned with getting the houses built than with the name of the park. A large grotto to the Blessed Virgin was set up in the Park and another was erected at the end of the Marino. I was reminded of them again when I heard Brendan Kennelly reading his lovely poem about Joyce dining with the

Holy Family in Nazareth. The Blessed Virgin asked if there were many grottoes to her in Ireland. Joyce assured her there were. We certainly did our bit in Blackrock.

I ran into trouble about the Blessed Virgin and my name as a small child. Some non-Protestant children who lived locally said I could not be called Mary after the Blessed Virgin Mary because Protestants did not believe in her. Now, I was very proud of being called Mary and particularly looked forward to nativity plays in which I felt, whether on stage or not, I had a leading role. Also, my mother was a member of the Mother's Union and there was a framed copy of the organisation's membership scroll in my parents' bedroom, featuring prominently the "Virgin and Child" by Murillo. "No," said my friends, "you must be called after Queen Mary of England." All I knew about Queen Mary of England were reports in the newspapers that if she came to tea it was a good idea to keep an eye on the teaspoons because she was a kleptomaniac! Perhaps she was being maligned, but she was not the sort of role model I sought.

Secondary school, Rochelle, was segregated too, from both a gender and denominational point of view. There were some Jewish girls and a few Roman Catholics who were the children of "mixed" marriages. The dreaded *Ne Temere* was very strictly enforced by Bishop Con Lucey. This led to the separation of young people in such a sad way, both religious groupings encouraging apartheid.

Bishop Con Lucey was an important person in my education about sex. Every year he would conduct confirmation services among his diocese and his homilies at these seemed to be mainly about sex and its associated sins. These sermons were reported in full in the *Cork Examiner* and any child who was curious could glean plenty of information from them about fornication, whatever that was. They were nearly as explicit as the reports of cases of "criminal conversation". When my own confirmation came about in the lovely St Finnbarre's Cathedral, it was a very tame affair compared to what went on in Clonakilty, Cloyne, etc.

Entering Protestant churches could cause trouble for Roman Catholics. Even if it was a cousin's wedding or funeral, the non-Protestants stayed outside. This stipulation caused great hurt to Protestants. I once heard Cardinal Cahal Daly, a man I much admire, say, when asked by the late Tom Fox TD at the Forum for Peace and Reconciliation if he thought it had not been a sad mistake, that he could not remember those times. Now I am a great deal younger than the Cardinal and I remember them well. At times of grief or joy, just when solidarity was needed most, friends and neighbours could not be there.

As children, we didn't go into the local Roman Catholic church much but we always made a pilgrimage to town each Christmas to look at the cribs. The best cribs were in the Franciscan Church in Washington Street and in the new church behind the Court House. Church of Ireland cribs were very poor in comparison, I suppose in case we got too involved in worshipping "graven images".

There was a large congregation of Methodists who attended Wesley Chapel in Patrick Street, too. My father was a Methodist and for some years we attended the Sunday school there. Methodist Sunday schools were by far the most fun and had the best outings. John Wesley seemed to have approved of a bit of *craic* as well as praying.

Protestant sales of work were a big thing. My mother always seemed to be raising money with cake and jam stalls for the Victoria Hospital, a Protestant institution now joined with the adjacent South Infirmary. The best lemon curd ever could be bought at these sales.

Collecting for the Mission to Lepers was another charitable task in which we were involved. My mother would select those from whom we could collect on the Castle Road and Menloe Park and Catholics were included. Indeed, interdenominational support for charities was the rule. St Vincent de Paul volunteers were thought very highly of in our home.

I went to Trinity rather than University College Cork. In the late 1950s, I think the efforts to make UCC an almost totally Roman Catholic college had been very successful and I would have been very isolated, as denominational religion featured heavily in universities then. We had family connection with Trinity, my father's cousin, Professor Robert Rowlette (who also represented Trinity in the Seanad) being one. The financial cost to my parents, who were not rich, must have been considerable. At this time, although when I went to Trinity I did not know it, Archbishop McQuaid had forbidden Roman Catholics from his diocese attending the place. Young people must now feel that such segregation only took place in Ireland in the days of the dodo but in fact it is but a few decades ago.

Working in the Rotunda as a young doctor, I became involved in the campaign to make contraception available in this country. My reasons were medical. Women were being denied the right to life because of their inability to limit the number of pregnancies they had.

I have never appealed for anything here to be changed for sectarian reasons but I have appealed frequently for changes on behalf of all Irish women. Read Austin Clarke's poem "The Redemptorist" and it is easy to see how frequently, alas, the position of the Roman Catholic Church and the lack of rights of women were intertwined.

There have been major changes in attitudes by the Christian denominations in Ireland but we have more to do. When will the 39 Articles be revisited? And what about interdenominational Holy Communion?

Anne Holliday

Anne Holliday was born in Limerick. She founded the Limerick and Clare chapter of the Irish Georgian Society in 1972, and worked on IGS restoration projects. She co-founded New Consensus, which organised peace pickets outside the Sinn Féin and UDA headquarters and promoted pluralist principles that were reflected in the Belfast Agreement. She was a founder member of the Peace Train Organisation, which opposed the IRA bombing of the Dublin–Belfast rail line. She lives in Dublin with her partner Michael Nugent and their ever-growing family of cats.

Confusing Identities

The special position of the Roman Catholic Church may be gone from the Irish Constitution, but not from the hearts and minds of many Irish citizens. When people use the word parish to describe an area of land, they mean the area covered by a Roman Catholic parish. Before I can watch the news, my State-funded television and radio service broadcasts the Angelus to me. As an inpatient in one of my State-funded hospitals, I hear priests saying the rosary, as they wander the public corridors beneath large statues of Mary and the crucified Jesus. I feel somehow excluded from the State of which I am proud to be a citizen, and I wonder how much more excluded do non-Christian citizens feel.

I grew up outside Limerick, in a family of Anglo-Irish heritage. I soon realised that we were different from our neighbours, most particularly on Poppy Day. Mummy sold poppies but only to a small group of people, almost like a secret society with a hidden identity. In the 1950s, when I was little more than a toddler, I saw neighbours shouting and spitting at mummy for trying to sell poppies. Later I learned about relatives and friends of my parents who had fought against the Nazis and been prisoners of war. I was astonished that this was a thing to be hidden, to be ashamed of. It was as if you ceased to be Irish if you had fought in either the Great War or the Second World War — but then you weren't properly Irish if you were Protestant, anyhow!

I went to a small Church of Ireland school. We wore quite a distinctive uniform, easily recognised. When I was 11, on walking home past a convent school, my friend and I were spat on and had dirt thrown at us, amid anti-Protestant songs and taunts. I was terrified. I would not walk past that school again for years. I had become self-conscious and confused about my identity.

My maternal grandfather was a Church of Ireland rector. My mother was born in 1922, during a pitched battle between the Treaty and anti-Treaty forces. The railway line from Limerick to their village had been blown up, so the doctor could not attend my grandmother, and she bled to death. My grandfather was nearly shot that year. He looked quite like Dev with his long nose, and only his silver cigarette case with his name engraved on it (a gift from parishioners) convinced the Free-Staters that he was not Dev in disguise. He had another escape when he was ordered to hand over his Union Flag from the rectory. He hid it in my aunt's nappy. That was a search too far and the flag survived.

In 1921, my paternal grandmother, an Englishwoman, was walking home from Limerick with my father and aunt in her pram, accompanied by their nurse. A truck drove by with Black and Tans shooting in all directions. My grandmother was shot in the thigh and, terrified and bleeding, she, the nurse and the two children escaped home through the swampy fields. Her attitude, and that of my parents, business people in Limerick, was "keep the head down, never draw attention to yourself, don't get involved and you will be alright". We were silent too long. It was almost as if we had disappeared along with those of us who had fled the new State.

In 1966, the people from "The Department" came to give picture books out at the schools and to talk about how brave and wonderful the 1916 leaders were. I had confusing nightmares of bleeding men in uniform, clutching rosary beads, being pounded to death by an army in which our grand uncles and cousins had bravely fought in the trenches of Flanders. And the "men in the mohair suits" started to destroy our eighteenth-century heritage, forgetting in their haste to erase the past that it was Irish men, craftsmen and architects, who had designed, built and lived in these magnificent buildings. Without the intervention of "the belted earls", as the Irish Georgian Society's founders were nick-named by a Fianna Fáil Minister, they might have succeeded.

In the 1980s, a prominent Fine Gael TD called Protestants "enemies of the people". During the 1998 Belfast Agreement referendum, some Fianna Fáil canvassers asked me to vote yes despite "the Protestants having shot, exiled and burned out our Catholic neighbours in the Six Counties". I asked them had this happened here. Thinking I was English by my accent, they assured me no. When I told them that the IRA had destroyed many of the great houses of Ireland, they said I was lying and indeed I was only wel-come in this country "if I thought like the people of this country".

Why, for so many years, have whole sections of the Irish popu-lation been written out of our history? Is it because we do not suit the idealised stereotype of the True Irish Roman Catholic Celtic Na-tionalist, a fiction created during the Celtic Revival in the second half of the nineteenth century, which would have excluded even Wolfe Tone? I love my country, and it *is* my country. I am proud of our cultural, literary, artistic, architectural and commercial heritage. Ireland is still a young State, which needs to come to terms with both its history and its rapidly changing country and population.

There is, of course, now a new group to be xenophobic about and they are rather easier to spot, with their different coloured skins, different languages and cultures. Yet this Ireland is their country too. Where once the Protestants and Jews were the minor-ity, now there are many minorities, each with the equal right to be treated with respect, as Irish citizens or residents. Their religions and cultures must also be respected, understood, and celebrated, as we embrace as Irish the evolving reality of our peoples.

David Kingston

David Kingston was brought up and went to school in Northern Ireland, where his father was a Church of Ireland clergyman. After three years in Oxford and four in Edinburgh, he moved with his wife to Dublin in 1968. He worked for 30 years with Irish Life, latterly as managing director. He is now a director of Dublin Network, an investment company. He has recently been President of the Faculty of Actuaries in Scotland and is currently Chairman of the Irish Stock Exchange. He is also actively involved with Trinity College and the Religious Society of Friends.

I was born in a small village in Northern Ireland nearly 60 years ago. Being Protestant pervaded everything in that life — school, church, politics, friends, economic prospects.

In the subsequent 60 years, all that has changed. Totally so in the Republic, where I have lived for the latter half of my life. Even in Northern Ireland, there has been major change.

In some ways, I have always been an outsider — something of a hybrid. My father was born in Wexford and never totally assimilated into being part of the Northern Ireland majority. When I went to work in England and then to Oxford, I realised that the English regarded me as Irish — not, as I thought, as one of their fellow UK citizens. My first boss — the manager of a beach café in Devon — insisted on calling me "Paddy"; the same thing had happened to two aunts of my wife a generation earlier. So during my time in England and Scotland, I became far more aware of being Irish and of living that persona. When I came to live in Dublin, some of the reverse opinions were there for a long time.

By 1968, I was definitely Irish in my own mind, reinforced by my marriage to a girl from Kildare. It was time to try out the real thing, to see if Ireland would live up to my romantic image.

And did it? Well it never could do so completely. Romantic dreams are never to be fully realised! In any event, dreams change with the practical experience of living and with the evolution of the society in which we live.

Rather than answering the "has the dream been fulfilled?" question directly, let me say something about how Ireland and I have fared over the last 30 years and how I see things today. When I left Scotland in 1968, I was warned that I was going to an economic backwater. True enough at the time, but not true today. Ireland in 1968 had started the evolutionary process of becoming an advanced economy, but it was not at all certain that it would succeed. In retrospect, the economic achievements of the last 30 years have been astonishing.

One of the key reasons for that success has been the capacity of Irish people to absorb the better parts of other economic cultures. This is easily said but very hard to achieve. At the time I came to Dublin to work in investment management, about half a dozen others who had worked abroad — people like Frank Fagan, Liam Jones and Frank Shanley — had also newly returned. Progressive companies like Irish Life and some stockbrokers absorbed us and let us apply our knowledge. It says a lot for Ireland that we were allowed to do this with nothing but encouragement.

And herein lies the fulfilment of one side of my romantic dream. I wanted to contribute to making Ireland a dynamic economy where there would be good jobs for all; I have been able to see this dream fulfilled.

Frankly, this has little to do with being Protestant. It is true that the Ireland of 1968 had lots of "Protestant" businesses, virtually none of which survive in that form today. But I joined Irish Life, a semi-state which hardly fitted that mould. Paradoxically, all the chief executives of Irish Life have been Protestant but this is more a tribute to the desire to get the best person for the job than any form of reverse discrimination.

The growth of the past 30 years is very largely a tribute to the framework set by Lemass and Whitaker in the early 1960s. No tribute in my mind can be high enough for these two men who framed an economic vision of a new Ireland which was based on no ideology other than good jobs for all.

Of course, this economic growth has itself been a driver of other changes. I was part of an interesting experiment in about 1985 when Paddy Harte founded an organisation called the Irish American Partnership. Paddy — a man of great vision — conceived the idea that the only way to resolve the north/south divide was to make the south at least as prosperous as the North. I have no doubt that the achievement of this goal has caused a huge change in the attitude of Northern business people and professionals to the south.

I have pointed to the capacity of people in the Republic to absorb the better economic ideas. Of course, this is associated with the absorption of social ideas as well. This has allowed people of all religions in the Republic to move to a different framework where one's religion is far less important in determining difference than it was.

I see this especially in institutions like Trinity and the MANCH Tallaght hospital. The mores which lie behind these institutions have changed over the past 30 years to become far more inclusive, allowing broad-minded people of all religious groups — and of none — to participate fully. This has been great for everyone involved.

Looking forward, it seems to me that the issues for the next 30 years are quite different. Can we use the examples of our overcoming religious problems to absorb new immigrants? Can we maintain some form of moral and religious values in a world where people no longer listen uncritically to Rome or Canterbury? Can we learn to deal with addictive substances like alcohol and drugs in a sensible manner? Can we continue the economic growth which seems necessary for society to behave generously to others? Can we create some greater sense of community?

I look forward to being part of this. I am no longer an outsider — my commitment to Ireland, to Europe and to the wider world is no different than that of most if not all Irish people. I have been lucky to be part of such an exciting period and to have been absorbed by such a fascinating society.

Archdeacon Gordon Linney

Archdeacon Gordon Linney was born in Dublin in 1939 and educated at the High School, Dublin. He began his working life at the Royal Bank of Ireland, 1957, but resigned to train for ordination in 1966. He was ordained at St Anne's Cathedral, Belfast in 1969, to serve in Portstewart, County Derry. He moved to St Patrick's Cathedral, Dublin, in 1975. He was appointed rector of Glenageary in 1980 and Archdeacon of Dublin in 1988.
He is a former Honorary Secretary of the General Synod of the Church of Ireland. He married Helen Henry in 1965. They have two married daughters, Susan and Heather, one son, David, and three grandchildren.

It would be too easy, from a minority point of view, to exaggerate the negative aspects of Irish life over the past century. Irish people, minorities included, have a tendency to see themselves as victims, rather like the hypochondriac who enjoys ill health!

But for members of the religious and political minority, life was difficult in the early decades of this State. In 1922, for example, the Archbishop of Dublin, Dr Gregg, publicly called upon the Government "to take the necessary steps to protect a grievously wounded minority . . . and to save the Protestants . . . from threatened violence and expulsion from their homes". In his diary, he refers to "news of evictions, ejections and intimidations everywhere". My parents' generation lived through those times and their memories and experiences inevitably became part of my story, but not the whole story.

Growing up in the environs of Inchicore Railway Works where my father worked was a great advantage, for we belonged first and foremost to a railway community, which to some extent had a life of its own. As children, we mixed with the other children living around us. But there were differences. We were members of the Church of Ireland. We were active in our local church and made our social contacts and friendships in church circles. So in a sense we withdrew into our minority shell and lost touch with the culture of the time, including its music and literature, isolated in an Anglo-Irish time warp.

It is important to recall the flavour of the 1930s and 1940s in Ireland. Economically, times were hard for most people and we were no exception. But the political and religious climate was especially difficult for minorities. The impression was given that being Irish meant being green nationalist/republican, Roman Catholic and anti-British. There was a certain inevitability about this, given the bitter divisions and conflicts of earlier years and centuries, assisted by a very one-sided treatment of history, but it created the climate in which "Prods" were viewed with suspicion and they kept their heads down with a few brave exceptions. In the Forum for Peace and Reconciliation at Dublin Castle some years ago, a senior Church of Ireland churchman, when asked to comment on this period, remarked that we had been "gently squeezed". I think it was more than that.

As a family we were hugely proud to be Irish, with roots going back many centuries. My father was a strong Redmond supporter who abhorred political violence. My mother, with Presbyterian origins in Armagh, had a unionist background but still considered herself to be Irish. There were strong family connections in Canada, the United States and Britain. During the Second World War, we had family members serving in all three armies, as others had done in the First World War, and we found it hard to see them disowned and dishonoured in the land of their birth or ancestry. This compounded our sense of isolation. I recall the annual Remembrance Day parade in the War Memorial Park at Kilmainham and the sadness felt when it was discontinued. At the same time, there was much remembering of those who had fought in the War of Independence and the Civil War, but no remembering of their victims. I have no difficulty understanding the political and historical aspects of these contrasting situations. I simply mention them as indicators of an attitude that nurtured a sense of polite exclusion and led many to feel that their future lay elsewhere than in Ireland. My two brothers left Ireland in the 1960s. They never returned.

The political climate did improve as the old Civil War tensions eased in the 1960s but since the Northern conflict erupted, there has been a drift back to the old green Catholic nationalist Ireland agenda originating north of the border. We seem unable to broaden our understanding of what it is to be Irish. Governments in recent years have aligned with Northern nationalism, which, as of old, excludes those with a different political outlook, including many members of the Church of Ireland. When Irish nationalism and republicanism speak of Irish America they mean Catholic Irish America and the Kennedys — the huge Irish American constituency of my tradition is ignored.

It is difficult for those who were not members of a religious minority to appreciate the smothering dominance of Roman Catholicism in the Ireland of my childhood and early adult years. A particular manifestation of this was the infamous *Ne Temere* decree, which in an inter-church marriage required that the non-Roman Catholic partner would agree to the children being brought up as Roman Catholics. *Ne Temere* not only decimated the Church of Ireland and other religious minorities but also divided families for generations. On a personal note, an inter-church marriage was never an issue. Yet, one generation later, my two daughters are happily married to Roman Catholics without any fuss. The challenge for the future will not be what denomination their children will be but whether they grow up as adult Christians in any denomination.

Inter-church difficulties were not all one-sided. There was (and is) a strong anti-Catholic bias in many Protestant minds and an inability to acknowledge the good things of that tradition. Too often we defined ourselves by what we were not rather than by what we were. This changed to some extent in the last quarter of the twentieth century when the Church of Ireland had to declare its position on such matters as family planning, divorce, abortion and the ordination of women and in doing so spoke for many outside its own membership. To this end, the media, especially television, have had an important role in explaining different sections of Irish society to each other.

The ecumenical movement has been very significant. It is difficult now to believe that when my father died in 1963, Roman Catholic friends of his were not allowed by their Church to attend his funeral service. Some did, but those who remained outside could not imagine the hurt they caused. I remember the first steps in ecumenical dialogue and the liberation that came with the discovery that we had so much in common. This has completely changed the religious scene at ground level, even though there are examples of intolerance to be found still. I came across them in the effort to bring Dublin's Adelaide Hospital into a new multi-denominational complex at Tallaght. Majorities sometimes fail to recognise that minorities deserve something more than a memorial plaque on a wall saying that they were once here. They want to have some say in building the future.

We have come a long way from the note of despair in Archbishop Gregg's 1922 diary and there is still a long way to go, especially in Northern Ireland. Our best hope lies not in the bland uniformity favoured by some but in the inclusive diversity which is the authentic Ireland of which my community is and wants to be a part.

Edna Longley

Edna Longley is a Professor of English at the Queen's University, Belfast. She was born Edna Broderick in Dalkey, south County Dublin. She has written widely on Irish literature and culture, particularly in relation to Northern Ireland. She has authored Poetry in the Wars, Louis MacNiece: A Study *and* The Living Stream: Literature and Revisionism in Ireland. *She is co-editor of the* Bloodaxe Book of Twentieth-Century Poetry from Britain and Ireland. *Her latest book is* Poetry and Posterity.

I am an accidental Protestant. My father, T.S. Broderick, Professor of Pure Mathematics at Trinity, was a Catholic, and I was baptised a Catholic. My mother, also a mathematician, was a Presbyterian from the west of Scotland. I was born in December 1940 not long before Archbishop McQuaid renewed the fiat against Catholics attending Trinity. My father, angered, chose Trinity over the Church. And, given the tiny Presbyterian population in Dalkey and south Dublin more generally, *faute de mieux* my sister and I became members of the Church of Ireland — Protestant as opposed to Catholic or Dissenter.

Yet "member" is overstating it. My parents' mixed marriage had been delayed by hostility from both families. This confirmed them as essentially secularists who never forced us to attend Church or Sunday school. I must have picked up agnosticism at an early age. Occasionally, a Presbyterian minister would visit my mother, but my father's reaction to any glimpsed dog-collar was to leap upstairs and hide in his study. We effectively lost our parents' religious traditions: my father distanced himself from his Irish hinterland which included a bishop and a distinguished nun.

Nor did we have C of I relations or ancestors — and religion is ancestral in Ireland or it is nothing. So it was school that turned us into "southern Protestants", school that socialised us into a world whose strangeness, narrowness and defensiveness I only realised in my late teens.

Like the other small Protestant schools that clung on in the 1940s and 1950s, Glengara Park (girls only) was closely allied with its parish church. We said prayers every morning. We had scripture lessons and joined the Scripture Union — I kept up the reading for a few masochistic weeks. We were prepared for Confirmation: somehow more an adolescent than theological rite of passage. We rehearsed assiduously for special church services. I was chosen to read "The people that walked in darkness . . ." at one carol service, and am glad to have absorbed great Anglican words and rhythms before the New English Bible cast its prosaic blight.

Some would call Glengara "west British". We played games every day, and one game was lacrosse. In November, we wore poppies. The headmistress, Miss Darling, used to warn us about the Soviet Threat. The school showed the film of Queen Elizabeth's Coronation. One girl objected. On St Patrick's Day, we weirdly mixed sport, religion and more localised patriotism by singing "St Patrick's Breastplate" before going out to play seven-a-side hockey in fancy dress. We thought it unfair that pupils in other schools could get extra marks in Inter and Leaving because they sat exams "through the medium". The necessity to learn Irish was accepted, but without ideological attachment. Earlier, I would feel invaded when, on certain Sundays, Irish dancers inexplicably took over Sorrento Park, my adventure playground.

In 1956, I went for two years to Alexandra College — then still facing, across Earlsfort Terrace, the alternative universe of UCD. Alexandra, with its distinguished record of promoting women's education, was more articulate than Glengara on its relation to Irish history and society. The Irish language mattered more. I heard the republican historian Dorothy Macardle (an alumna) speak there shortly before she died. Yet it was also there that a clergyman from the North spent a scripture lesson urging us not to forget the doctrinal "differences between 'us' and our Roman Catholic fellow-countrymen". Perhaps my own mixed background makes me remember the occasion.

So where, meanwhile, was Catholic Ireland? For me, it was largely the hidden Ireland — as doubtless the south Dublin Protestant micro-world was to it. My father obviously had Catholic friends: indeed, his friendship with Monsignor Patrick Browne was significant for Trinity's involvement in setting up the Institute for Advanced Studies. But he, like my mother, was shy, and this made the school/church milieu all the more encompassing. southern Protestant teenage life in the mid 1950s revolved around church youth clubs and church-hall "hops". The fear that mixed marriages would further shrink the community impelled C of I efforts to control the young. I had once played with Catholic children who lived nearby, but less and less as the mutual imperative of segregation took hold. I missed them.

Of course, class came into it. The Dalkey of Hugh Leonard's *Home Before Night* is largely alien to my experience. My Dalkey was full of Protestant spinsters or widows who ran market-gardens — now swept away by time, rock stars and film directors. Yet class operated *within* southern Protestantism too. I also missed a girl whose posher parents removed her from Glengara to send her to boarding-school in England. My father may have been a TCD professor, but his salary was low. We didn't own our house or have a car. When I went to Trinity I felt intimidated by the upper-class English students. Yet, like the Northern Protestants I first met in numbers, Brendan Kennelly (in whom Catholic Ireland came out of hiding), and other exotics, those foreigners changed the horizon.

Vivian Mercier summed up the boredom of his Protestant teens in a small Irish town when he said: "there was just me and a girl the same age, and we were sick looking at one another". It may have been unconscious boredom, as well as my underlying sense of being slightly outside the southern Protestant ethos, that produced some kind of inner resistance. Although as shy as my parents, around 1958 I took part in a debate on the proposition "That the minority do not play their full part in the affairs of the Republic of Ireland". I found my paper for this debate — I attacked both the Republic and the minority — inside a 1944 copy of *The Bell*. This contains an article I must have consulted: W.B. Stanford, the TCD Professor of Greek (who lived up the road), writing on the exclusion of southern Protestants from public life. The article drew a "Proddy lie down" riposte from Sean O'Faoláin. Was it exclusion, self-exclusion or self-seclusion? Today the Northern Protestant community can similarly behave like a rolled-up hedgehog — an image once used of Northern Catholics.

When I read Hubert Butler's classic essay "Portrait of a Minority", I identified with his satirical analysis and prophetic anxiety: "So now our amiable inertia, our refusal to express grievances or cherish hopes about Ireland, are really delaying our ultimate unity and the reconciliation of our two diverging communities." Butler healthily broke interdenominational taboos and "rocked the boat". There is sometimes a fine line between boat-rocking and coat-trailing, but it's better to be damned if you do than damned if you don't. This also applies to rocking boats *within* faith communities — as in the Church of Ireland over Drumcree. Nobody will ever convince me that the ethnic-territorial divergence in Ireland is not religiously based. The absence of universal integrated education disgraces Church and State. In adulthood, I finally met people I should have met in childhood. But it took longer for us to learn each other's language — if we wanted to, that is.

My father died in 1962. The Catholic church in Dalkey buried him, and de Valera (who used to ring him up about mathematics) came to the funeral. Afterwards, the parish priest caught me outside our house: "Have you ever thought about religion?" With surprising presence of mind, I replied: "No, I'm more interested in literature." This interest, variously, took me to Belfast in 1963. And that's how I became an accidental Northerner.

Gillian Lyster

Gillian Lyster was born in Dublin in 1943. She was educated in Longford and Dublin. She is married and has three sons, and lives in south County Dublin where she is involved with her local community, Church, and musical society.

I have happy memories of growing up in the midlands of Ireland during the 1940s and 1950s. My family lived on the outskirts of a county town, where my father ran a business. I imagine our town would have been fairly typical with its schools, churches, shops, pubs, banks, post office, cinema, hospital, etc.

Catholic and Protestant children were educated separately in those days, so I had my early education at the Church of Ireland primary school. My Catholic friends would have gone to the local convent or to the boys' school.

The two "persuasions" did keep to themselves to a certain extent but in my opinion we always had great respect and affection for each other. One of the things which helped to unite us all was music. My mother was a professional musician and our town was privileged to have a very good Musical Society of which she was a member. Each year, the Society would present a light opera or musical comedy and this gave enormous fun and enjoyment to a wide section of the community. I remember *Oklahoma* farmers and cowmen practising their song-and-dance routine in our drawing-room until the wee small hours, my father beginning to wonder if they had no homes to go to. The production might run for up to two weeks and sometimes included Sundays. When Sundays were included, an understudy would step into my mother's role.

Sunday for our family was a special day spent in a different way to the other days of the week. We would go to church in the morning and sometimes again in the evening. Lunch would be a more elaborate meal than on weekdays and we would take more time to enjoy it together. After lunch, we would relax and read or perhaps take a walk in the country, but we would never have gone to the cinema or any place of public entertainment.

Handel's *Messiah* brought the two "persuasions" together when members of the Cathedral joined with members of the Church of Ireland choir to sing this wonderful work. The bass rank was a bit short of voices, so the bank manager's wife joined in and sang the low notes beautifully!

I don't remember how it came about but two of my school friends and I took piano lessons at the convent. I think the nuns may have been a bit shocked when we turned up for our lessons wearing shorts and T-shirts. We meant no offence; this would have been quite acceptable summer attire at our school, where we didn't have any particular uniform.

The convent offered the only secondary education for girls in our town so my parents sent me away to a coeducational board-ing school in Dublin where my father had been educated. I spent six happy years there, returning to the country for school holi-days. It was always wonderful to get home for holidays and have time to catch up with other friends. One of the exciting events which took place during the holidays was the parish "social". A social, for those who have never heard of such a thing, was an evening of ballroom dancing and supper in the parish hall. Great fun would be had by those of us who helped prepare the hall and make the sandwiches, etc. There would be much speculation about who would come on the night!

Our church hosted a choral festival when singers would come from neighbouring parishes to sing together. I always enjoyed the music so much. We were fortunate to have a good organist and many good voices. The harvest festival was another great annual event which took place in late September or early October. On the Friday night, there would be a harvest thanksgiving service in the church and it would include wonderful hymns and anthems. Afterwards, everyone went across to the parish hall for supper and a dance. The harvest service was repeated on the Sunday morning. There was a Methodist church in our town where my grandfather had been the minister many years ago. The Methodists had a harvest thanksgiving service at which the children from the Church of Ireland primary school would be invited to sing. I remember their lovely organist pedalling furiously to keep the harmonium pumped up while we tried to sing and keep our giggles under control. She always called us "doties", which was a term of endearment we probably didn't deserve.

One of the memories of our domestic scene was "Fridays". My mother had a wonderful woman who came to help her in the house a couple of days a week and Friday was one of her days. For the majority of people, fish was the order of the day on Friday at that time, so fish was what we had. I remember to this day the smell of smoked haddock and having to be so careful not to swallow the bones.

During my last year at boarding school, my mother died quite suddenly. Our family was devastated. I remember the vice-principal coming to my classroom to take me to the headmaster's office, where my brother was waiting to tell me the terrible news. I often wonder if I would have taken a different path through life if my mother had been here to guide me — who knows? I had a wonderful relationship with my father and he always gave me the best possible advice when I needed it. Sadly, in those days, many of my mother's very dear friends who would have wanted to attend her funeral were not permitted to enter our church. Thankfully, that ridiculous situation has been changed and we can all now support each other in times of grief and on happy occasions.

In the 1960s, my life began to change. I finished school and college and started my first job in Dublin. Life was very different in the city. I played hockey for my old school club and we would play our matches on Saturdays. It became more and more difficult to compete with other clubs because a lot of the fixtures would take place on Sundays. I remember attending a meeting when it was decided that the club would have to take on a new name and drop the old school name so that the teams could play matches on a Sunday.

I was introduced to my husband, by a fellow with whom I had been at boarding school, at one of the famous "socials" in Dublin. We had our wedding in my country church where my mother's choral festival friends came and raised the roof for us. The Dublin guests were very impressed but I had to confess to them that it wasn't the regular church choir.

My three sons grew up in Dublin in the 1970s and 1980s and believe that I had a deprived childhood in the country compared with their life in the city. I must say, I was perfectly happy with my lot!

May McClintock

May McClintock (née Bonner) lives in New Mills, Letterkenny, County Donegal. Educated at the Prior School, Lifford, and the Church of Ireland Training College, Kildare Street, Dublin, she worked as a teacher for 45 years before her retirement in 1997. She is vice-president of Donegal Historical Association, secretary of Letterkenny Irish Farmers' Association and chairman of Donegal An Taisce Association. She has written a number of books on local history and flora, including After the Battering Ram: the Story of the Dispossessed in Derryveagh, Seedtime and Harvest: the History of Agriculture in East Donegal, *and* The Heart of the Laggan. *She is married to John McClintock M.RCV.S and they have two sons, two daughters and seven grandchildren.*

I was not aware of the term Ulster-Scot during my childhood, but I was keenly aware of my religion. Not everyone had a great-grandmother who entered in the religious profession on the 1901 Census "a saved sinner" while a daughter was more specifically "a sinner saved by grace". Growing up in the 1930s, I was surrounded by sinners, saved and unsaved, and nurtured on the Bible. At an early age I could quote Isaiah 53 and St John Chapter 3. A letter to my school read "our children are not to be taught any Catechism or the Creed". But it would be a very dull child in a one-teacher school who would not pick up information, especially if it was forbidden. The furore in my home is still a clear memory when I asked my grandfather, "Why did Jesus go to hell?" "Where did you hear that? Don't ever repeat that again." Another letter to the teacher.

First term in secondary school required participation in the nativity play. My first entry into a real church, with angels and candles, organ music and carols, was a revelation. It was my road to Damascus, an escape from fundamentalism.

My first teaching job was in a small one-roomed Presbyterian school in an area dominated by the Faith Mission. Children and parents attended evening services in a Mission Hall and, once a year, young female preachers known as Pilgrims visited the parish. They wore little black bonnets. I wonder if such a sect still survives. It was the time of Billy Graham and for my 21st birthday the children gave me a copy of his book. I remember an essay written by one of the pupils which began, "I want to be a Pilgrim when I grow up. I don't want to be like my teacher, she is going to hell." So once again I was back in an enclosed order, where sinners were closely monitored.

The manager was a devout Presbyterian minister who arranged living accommodation in the home of one of his aged parishioners, invited me to visit his manse and to socialise with his teenage children. Parish socials were the only form of entertainment. Dancing was not allowed — no bodily contact. I later heard of another parish where weekly sessions were held. To ensure that dancing could not take place, the local Garda sat in to monitor the situation. The organiser devised a brilliant plan — she invited the Garda to the kitchen for a specially prepared meal. During his absence, the dancing began.

During my childhood, the only Roman Catholics I was aware of were workmen, mostly hired, who worked on the farms. They smoked Woodbines, went to football matches and danced on the Sabbath. They even played cards and were to be avoided. During my second year as a teacher, I made a spur of the moment decision to leave the landlady and move into the hotel owned and run by a Catholic family. I was unaware that my decision would cause problems. No longer was I invited to the manse or the church socials and I was replaced by another Sunday school teacher. But it was a great decision, one that I have never regretted.

The hotel family were deeply religious, which showed in every aspect of their lives. Sundays and Feast days were strictly observed, bare-footed patterns were made to the holy well, the rosary recited every night by everyone in the hotel, except me. I was never invited. The walls were adorned with pictures of the saints, the Sacred Heart, the Pope, the Eucharistic Congress and the family at various religious celebrations. In my own house there were only embroidered pictures of Biblical quotations. The one above my bed during my childhood read, "Be still and know that I am God". I wasn't sure if this was a comfort or a threat.

During my years at the hotel I was aware and conscious of the daily religious obligations of the family — conscious but apart. My extremely kind landlady never let me forget that I was a Protestant, that I was different. A general election was due, my first occasion to vote. A small son in the household asked me who was I going to vote for; his mother was shocked: "Don't ask a question like that, she will be voting for her own man." Not knowing who my own man was, I made discreet inquiries — there was a Protestant candidate.

Years later, religion played a part in my entry to political life. On the resignation of a local authority councillor, I was selected by my party to fill the vacancy. At a council meeting, this co-option was on the agenda. The chairman's speech expresses how he felt "confident she would make an excellent Councillor". They had a predominantly nationalist council and they were co-opting a member of the minority; he continued: "I hope it goes out from here to her co-religionists across the border, to the Ulster-Scots, that they need have no fear to come into the Republic. We are a tolerant council co-opting a Protestant and this should nail the notion of those who say the minority do not have a fair deal here." He referred to the part played by Tone, McCracken, and Issac Butt in building up the nation and appealed to Protestants to play their part to have Tone's dreams realised. The next speaker said, "Mr Chairman, many are already playing their part; I don't agree with a lot of that bunk in your last few sentences." A friend in London who obviously read the local papers sent a telegram:

"Welcome to this great republican body." It was often pointed out to me that I held a unionist seat on the Council.

These reflections may help to explain some aspects of the way the Ulster-Scots are perceived. The Irish are not a pure race — those that claim to be Irish are a mixture of Celt and pre-Celt, of Viking and Norman, English, Huguenot and Palatine. They have become assimilated into our culture, whereas the Ulster-Scots have retained a separate identity, whether through choice, fear or intimidation. Those who have made some effort and tried to raise their heads are quickly identified as a betrayer of Protestantism by their own people and an intruder by those who espouse single-stream nationalism.

Ian McCracken

Ian McCracken is a member of the St Johnston Presbyterian Church. He was a physics teacher for nearly 40 years until his retirement in 1998. He is currently Community Development Officer for Donegal with Derry and Raphoe Action.

I was born in County Donegal in the year the giant airship *Hindenburg* exploded and the *Dandy* comic was born. Airships have been superseded by modern aircraft, while I understand on good authority the *Dandy* is still going. Apart from my time boarding in Sligo Grammar and High School, my four years in Trinity and one year in Mountjoy — teaching in the Mountjoy School in Dublin — I have lived my life to date in Donegal. Born into a Presbyterian home, I have continued in that religious denomination and am regular in my church attendance in St Johnston.

I taught physics for 38 years and was fortunate to have done a job which I enjoyed immensely. On my retirement from teaching in 1998, I enjoyed further good fortune when I was appointed to my present work as Development Officer in Donegal with Derry and Raphoe Action. This is a project managed by a voluntary committee with a mission to encourage Protestant participation in community development processes in mainly rural areas in counties Derry, Tyrone and Donegal — essentially, the Church of Ireland Diocese of Derry and Raphoe. The project owes its existence to the tremendous vision of Canon Bill McNee and the former Bishop James Mehaffy who recognised that the Protestant community was not availing of the great opportunities possible through the EUSSPPR. All observations and opinions which follow are personal and relate to Protestantism within Donegal.

The obvious question about the relative inactivity of Protestants is "Why?" Through my work, I have experienced some of the reasons for this. Attitudes can be influenced by situations. A look at the census figures for the years in which religious affiliations were examined is instructive.

Population Changes in Donegal, 1991–2002

Year	Total	R.C.	C of I	Pres	Meth.	Other	Total Prot	% of total
1891	185,635	142,893	21,884	18,055	2,006	797	**41,945**	**22.6**
1901	173,722	135,029	19,908	16,212	1,828	745	**37,948**	**21.8**
1911	168,537	133,021	18,020	15,016	1,698	768	**34,734**	**20.6**
1926	152,508	124,941	13,774	12,162	1,202	428	**27,138**	**17.8**
1936	142,310	118,906	11,516	10,445	1,042	387	**23,003**	**16.2**
1946	136,317	116,262	9,869	8,982	829	374	**19,680**	**14.4**
1961	113,842	98,252	7,345	7,173	734	192	**15,252**	**13.4**
1971	108,344	93,330	6,818	6,030	651	193	**13,499**	**12.5**
1981	125,112	108,988	6,464	5,806	613	233	**12,883**	**10.3**
1991	128,117	111,427	6,157	5,412	603	866	**12,172**	**9.5**

In Donegal, as in the rest of the Republic of Ireland during the twentieth century, total numbers fell steadily. This trend reversed in the total population of Donegal in the inter-census period 1971–81. Protestant numbers continued to fall, although more slowly. Numbers of communicant members from some Protestant Churches have indicated at least a halt in this decline, if not a small increase. Most starkly, the proportion of Protestants to the total population in the county has shown a steady decline from 22.6 per cent to 9.5 per cent in 1991.

There is a great diversity within Protestantism. A recent count of the number of denominations of Protestantism within Northern

Ireland reached 53 — only just short of the number of Heinz varieties! Diversity is enriching, but if numbers are too small to make some activities viable, then it can lead to isolation and stagnation.

As numbers of Protestants decline, the financial demands on families and individuals increase. There are fewer contributors to maintain ageing Church buildings and fewer participants to engage in social and recreational activities in church halls. In my own St Johnston/Carrigans area the population is about 1,500 people. There are six Protestant church buildings for the 600 or so Protestants and two for the 900 Catholics of our community. This is replicated many times over throughout the county.

In the early 1960s, the hire purchase system allowed people to own household goods without having all the money to pay for them at the time. Because of the independent nature of Protestantism, there was little uptake from Protestants. "I'll get it when I can pay for it" was, and is, a common Protestant ethic. This individualistic ethos pervades the Protestant psyche — personal pews, personal responsibility, personal salvation.

Declining numbers, schism and fragmentation, the ethos of individualism, all these factors have contributed to the low level of Protestant community involvement. There has been a fear of losing what we have, of assimilation, if we are open to the wider community. There has been a reluctance to apply for grant aid, a "keep the head down" attitude that has led to a lack of confidence and a diminished capacity to engage. Perceptions prevented individuals applying for posts — the "I wouldn't get the job anyway" attitude. Protestants have largely excluded themselves from the opportunities that are available. This can be mistaken for deliberate withdrawal and interpreted as snobbish.

Our National Development Plan has put in place many measures for social inclusion. There is a growing confidence and level of expectation within all our people. There a realisation amongst our Protestant folk that positive community involvement and active citizenship is one way of retaining our identity and securing a future as part of a cohesive community.

Protestants have played a significant role in the birth and growth of our State, Dr Douglas Hyde being the first President. Protestants made major contributions to the survival of the Irish language in the eighteenth and nineteenth centuries. People such as Henry Joy McCracken, his sister Mary Ann, Henry Munroe and Robert McAdam were very active in preserving Gaelic language and culture. Indeed, the Presbyterian Church at the end of the nineteenth century demanded that candidates for the ministry should be able to converse in Irish — the only denomination at that time to do so. Protestants of today have, I believe, an important role to play in a modern multicultural Ireland. We cannot make that contribution unless we opt in to the changes that are happening at a great pace in every aspect of society. We have a rich diversity of culture to share. We also have much to learn about sharing resources within our Protestant traditions as well as in our wider communities.

The circumstances that led to most individuals' places in the local community are largely dictated by past events. I would compare this brief look at Protestants in Donegal to a walk along a stony beach. The majority of the stones are from the local geological rock formation and are shaped and rounded by the forces of the relentless pounding of the waves. However, here and there are stones of a different colour that have been swept in from other places. They add variety and interest to the shore. Not only does the relentless rise and fall of the tide shape the stones, it also shapes the coastline where they lie. So too in our communities, there are forces that shape and mould us as individuals as well as the communities in which we live. We should see the enriching value of those who are different and strive to have some influence on the way we interact and have an input into our relationships to one another. Our common Christian heritage obliges us to do so.

Patsy McGarry

*Patsy McGarry has been Religious Affairs Cor-
respondent at* The Irish Times *since 1997.
From Ballaghaderreen, County Roscommon, he
has been in journalism since 1983 when he began working in the newsroom at the then Dublin
pirate station Sunshine Radio. Subsequently he
freelanced with the* Sunday World, Magill
*magazine, RTE, and the Irish Press group where
he was theatre critic from 1991 to 1996. In 1989,
he set up the first independent radio newsroom
in Ireland at Capital Radio in Dublin (now FM 104). He also worked
with Independent Newspapers and won a Journalist of the Year Award
in 1992 for comment and analysis with the* Sunday Independent. *He
was awarded the John Templeton European Religion Writer of the Year
Award in 1998.*

Pleasant if Potential Murderers

My own background is in the majority Roman Catholic tradition. But within that tradition my family, for generations,
would have belonged to those who were deeply suspicious of
clericalism, by which I mean the manner in which authority was
exercised by our priests and bishops.

I remember my grandfather, also Patsy McGarry, as an old
man playing "The Blackbird of Avondale" on a tin whistle and
weeping as he remembered the death of Parnell. He was in his
eighties by then and had not forgiven the Catholic bishops for the
part he believed they played in the downfall of the "Uncrowned
King of Ireland". He was also a quiet and gentle man, not at all
given to anger or tears. So the sight of his upset had a profound
impact on my young mind.

Gentle as he was, he was also very clear on where he stood as regards religion. He was a quietly prayerful man close to his God. It did not stop him, though, from challenging the local parish priest. The tradition at the time was that the priest would visit a selected house in a townland and say Mass to which all the neighbours were invited. The practice was known as "the stations". The stations came to a neighbour's house and my grandfather was there. As usual on such occasions, preparations continued to the last minute with new curtains being put up and furniture being freshly painted.

The priest arrived and Mass began. He began his sermon. At the time in the early 1930s a general election was taking place and the priest was a very political man. He told the people who they should vote for and why. My grandfather supported another candidate. He did the imponderable. He interrupted the priest and asked, pertinently, "Father, where does it say that in the Gospel?" The priest was apoplectic and denounced my father for his impertinence in challenging a man of God. Eventually, the Mass proceeded. At its end my grandfather tried to rise to leave, but could not get out of his chair. He tried again and again, finally breaking free. His more mischievous friends put about the rumour that he had been stuck to the chair for challenging the priest. And no doubt there were simple souls there at the time who would have believed that. In fact, he was stuck because the chair had only been painted that morning and it was still wet when he sat on it.

He and my father and, later, myself lived in the same house near Frenchpark in north-west Roscommon as my great-grandfather and great-great-grandfather had. Indeed, my great-grandfather, Paddy or Patsy McGarry also, had built that house with his own hands. Douglas Hyde grew up about four miles from our house. My father and grandfather remembered him with great respect, because they were deeply patriotic Irish nationalists. My father was a fervent member of the Gaelic League, which Hyde had founded. Hyde had learned his Irish and collected the material for his books from the people in the area that made up our world. He had created a national identity from such material.

It gave the people of our area a sense of pride when they realised this and, through him, their central part in the creation of the Irish nationalist identity and the new Irish State. Those people who were described in one book I read about Hyde as "so many pleasant if potential murderers". Such were my ancestors.

So when Hyde died in 1949, my father was among those locals who attended his burial at Portahard, a few miles from our house, despite the teaching of the Roman Catholic Church at the time that to do so — to even enter any Reformed Church — was to risk eternal damnation. That threat was enough to frighten the Government of the day to sit in their State cars outside St Patrick's Cathedral in Dublin during Hyde's funeral service. I am glad to say I come from stock made of sterner stuff, people who trusted that a merciful God would not damn them for accompanying a neighbour they were proud of on his last journey in this world.

There were very few people of the Reformed faith in our part of the world and those that were mainly came from small farming stock like the rest. The few families I knew were almost a protected species, with a certain exotic air to them. It would be true to say they were looked out for by their Catholic neighbours.

In the 1960s, we moved to Ballaghaderreen, just a few miles the other side of Hyde's home. There was just one Church of Ireland family in the town then; they were the local doctor's family and, by coincidence, the son of the family sat next to me at the local De La Salle Brother's school.

Stephen inspired much envy among us, his classmates. He didn't have to be in for the morning prayers. He could leave while the Angelus was being said and, above all, he didn't have to be there for Catechism class. He also didn't have to go to Mass on Sundays or evening devotions during Lent, May and November.

As well as being the only non-Roman Catholic boy in the school, he was the only one who wore braces on his teeth. We felt sorry for him on both counts, especially the more pious amongst us who believed we should be extra nice to him as he wasn't going to heaven, no matter what he did.

As I grew older, I became more aware of the minority position of people of the Reformed faith in this State and what this had meant for them. In particular, I became angered at the effects of the 1907 *Ne Temere* decree on that community, and the manner in which the then Article 44 of the Constitution — recognising the special position of the Catholic Church in this State — was used to bolster that decree in the civil law of the land.

In 1988, I wrote two lengthy articles for *Magill* magazine, one detailing the experience of the Church of Ireland community in this State up to that point. It was, if I may say so, very sympathetic. The other article was about Douglas Hyde and a detailed account of his seminal contribution to the existence of the Irish nationalist tradition and indeed the very existence of the State itself.

Indeed, this latter point got me thrown out of a presentation course at RTÉ. There was an argument raging at the time about the use of regional accents on RTÉ. I was very much in favour of the latter, but the woman in charge of our course — which was to be our entrée to the world of broadcasting — was utterly opposed. She favoured the retention of the standard "areTÉ" accent.

Coming to the end of the course, in a three-minute piece to microphone which each course participant had to do, I argued for regional accents on our airwaves but also suggested that if there was to be a standard accent on RTÉ, then it ought to be the Ballaghaderreen one. My argument was that the BBC standard Oxford accent had been a regional one too until the influence of the University there spread throughout English society. And what more worthy regional accent was there in Ireland than that of Douglas Hyde, who had "created" the Irish nationalist identity — which led to the Rising of 1916, the War of Independence, the creation of this State and Radio Éireann itself — before he became Ireland's first president! Such wonderful logic was lost on "the-woman-in-charge" at RTÉ, who threw me off the course with just two weeks to go. I shall be grateful, forever.

I would subscribe to Yeats' description of his and the Anglican tradition in Ireland as being of "no petty people". From Berkeley, through Grattan, Edward Fitzgerald, Robert Emmet, Thomas

Davis, John Mitchel — who was married in Drumcree church — through Isaac Butt, Parnell, Hyde, not to forget Yeats himself, Lady Gregory, John Millington Synge, Sean O'Casey, Lennox Robinson, etc., etc. . . . they have been giants of our history.

I am well aware of the socio-economic-historical factors that made this possible; the privileged status such people held in Irish society then, as members of the established Church, as well as the penal laws which enforced poverty, ignorance and exclusion on the great majority. But those people named above had all acted on behalf of the downtrodden majority. They had chosen to do so at great and frequently terrible cost to their own welfare. They had done so out of the highest motives of conscience. And they had done so for my people. My ancestors. My "pleasant if potential murderers".

As my father felt towards Hyde and my grandfather towards Parnell, I feel only gratitude to members of the Church of Ireland who played such a huge role in liberating my majority from one form of tyranny. And, as with my father and grandfather, I deeply regret that we allowed another form of tyranny replace it — a tyranny, in many cases of the "beggar on horseback" variety — at whose hands the Church of Ireland community, and others of the Reformed faith generally, were to suffer greatly, despite their enormous contribution to Irish nationalism and the existence of this State.

Despite my own disillusionment with both of the latter.

Senator Martin Mansergh

Martin Mansergh was elected to Seanad Éire-
ann in the 2002 elections. He was formerly Spe-
cial Adviser to the Taoiseach on Northern
Ireland, Economic and Social Matters. He stud-
ied at Oxford University where he became an
expert on eighteenth-century French history.
He is married to a Scotswoman and runs the
family farm in Tipperary with his brother.

The days of a self-conscious or nervous minority are past.
Many of the Protestant community still come together in
church on Sundays, but its members are now part of the mainstream of Irish life, their role no longer identified by their religious background. This was not always so, but the integration
achieved over a period of two generations is a tribute both to Irish
society as a whole and to the commitment of those who stayed (or
came) post-independence.

The precarious situation at the outset cannot be judged without reference to history. Three hundred years before, newcomers
took the lion's share of land, wealth and power in Ireland, at a
time of terrible deprivation among the people, in the expectation
that they would guarantee Britain's strategic control. In a later age
of democracy and nationalism, without the consent of the people,
neither minority rule nor British rule could indefinitely be sustained. While notable individuals and families identified with and
on occasion led or inspired the national movement to independence, a majority, believing British protection to be secure, actively

or passively formed an obstruction as long as they could to the separate emergence of a national democracy in Ireland.

Ulster unionism, which was stronger because geographically more concentrated, was brilliantly successful in its rearguard action, not least because it ruthlessly separated its interests from the rest. The revolution in Ireland from 1916 to 1923 found a scattered minority in the south and west vulnerable and defenceless, a minority whose natural leaders had badly misplayed a once-strong hand. Fortunately, most of the abuses, monopolies in church, land ownership and local government had already been reformed.

In the turmoil of the Troubles, the survival of the community depended more on its relationships with its neighbours and a willingness to accept a constructive attitude to the new powers in the land. Many left, voluntarily or otherwise, and while some lives were lost, attacks focused more on property, and even then most big houses survived or were rebuilt. I believe, contrary to some historians and journalists, that, in all the circumstances, the community could have fared a lot worse in a traumatic period, and that the Republican authorities tried to deal justly.

The new leaders of the south, recognising that, in the short term at least, much of the wealth of the country was still in the hands of a minority and not wanting to worsen the economic dislocation by driving it away, moved to provide reassurance, being able to cite individual contributions to independence and the ideals of Tone and Davis. Loyalty was transferred to the new State, even if old habits were slow to die, and initially the Senate provided honorary participation. Institutionalised land redistribution, the encouragement of native industry and generational change gradually whittled away the economic and social imbalances common to newly independent States. But for a while, a fairly sheltered existence continued in a lower key, with the country life, plentiful and affordable staff, low crime and low taxes proving highly attractive to wealthy settlers from a Britain and Europe that had been ravaged by the Second World War. The fall in numbers was partly stemmed by additions from outside.

Toleration fitted into an understanding of democracy, where the ethos of the majority was to prevail. There nevertheless existed a limited cultural and intellectual space, in which other elements in society took part, which in some respects was not immediately or entirely subject to the orthodox parameters of Church and State.

There were missed opportunities on all sides. Independent Ireland, while behaving honourably for the most part, was slow to see that the minority, in which it perceived a former and to some degree alien ruling class being treated better than it deserved, could contribute to the resolution of the problem in Northern Ireland. By the time the Troubles arrived post-1969, it lacked the critical mass to be a persuasive argument. On the side of the minority, there was a tendency to keep the head down, not just out of prudence, as has often been claimed, but because few wanted to get into the awkward implications of confronting the ethical issues of the past or expressing regret from a position of weakness.

What the renewed Troubles post-1969 demonstrated early on was how far in 50 years the paths of the co-religionists North and south had diverged. Few wanted to risk the relative harmony here on account of the disharmony in the North, so people drew closer together.

Over the past 40 years, Ireland as a society has opened up far more. Ecumenism led to greater mutual religious respect and an acceptance that people have far more in common than what divides them. The traditional social inequalities and class divisions became less marked. Ireland gained steadily in self-confidence, through its EEC/EU membership, growing economic prosperity, sporting and cultural achievements, and eventually through the establishment of peace in Ireland. Separate religious institutions were on the decline, but participation in everything on the increase. Ireland has always been a fine country. Now it was becoming a prosperous and successful one, in which every citizen could take pride. Unobtrusively, many old wounds were healed, as a broader, more pluralist sense of identity became established.

Not everyone is pleased at the successful integration of an independent Ireland. A united Ireland continues to be portrayed by many unionists as a mortal threat to the Protestant identity, even though independence is not experienced that way in the south. There have been limited efforts, with little support, to canvass a separate political/cultural and more assertively pro-British minority identity in the aftermath of the Good Friday Agreement. Ireland's greater European and global involvement today and its growing multicultural character in any case transcend the differences in background derived from the often claustrophobic history of the two islands. Rethinking independence is not a plausible option. Joining fully in making the most of independence is.

Bishop Michael Mayes

The Right Reverend Michael H.G. Mayes is Bishop of Limerick and Killaloe. Apart from a four-year curacy in Portadown followed by almost seven years in Japan, his entire ministry has been in the Republic, first as a parochial clergyman and later an archdeacon in Cork, then as a bishop in Kilmore in Cavan, and now in Limerick.

This essay is not to be seen as representing the official views of the Church of Ireland in general, or of the Diocese of Limerick and Killaloe of which I happen to be bishop. Still less is it a historical assessment of the fortunes of the Church of Ireland. It is purely personal, reflecting on one person's experiences of life in the Republic of Ireland.

I was born in County Derry during the Second World War of a very English mother, a doctor (Cheltenham Ladies' College, London University and the Royal Free Hospital) and an Irish father, who, like many members of his family, was a clergyman and product of TCD. I was schooled in the village of Benburb in County Tyrone and the Royal School, Armagh, and am a graduate of Trinity College, Dublin, and later of the University of London.

Inevitably this kind of background will produce a certain confusion of outlook, where life is not seen to be nearly as clear-cut as many people would like it to be. This does not always go down well with those who prefer their bishops to be very firm and clear in their pronouncements. My mother was determined that her children should see that there is more than one side to the Eternal Irish Question, and the years in a Buddhist/Shinto religious environment forced me to see that the very phrase "the eternal truths of the Gospel" frequently indicates a high degree of cultural arrogance, usually unwitting, on the part of those who use it.

My first experience of life in the Republic of Ireland was as a 17-year old student at TCD in 1958. Looking back on those days, my abiding reaction is one of almost unbelieving astonishment at the way Ireland has changed in the space of one generation. We could be living on two different planets. Forty-something years ago, God was in Heaven, John Charles McQuaid was in Dublin, and between them all was well with the Irish world. The soul of Ireland was in safe hands, as long as the Irish people, from the Taoiseach down, adhered to the paths of truth and righteousness as prescribed by God and John Charles. The troublesome Noel Brownes of Irish society were given short shrift and kept firmly in their place.

In my first or second year in Dublin, I witnessed a Corpus Christi procession. I had done Latin in school and could at least translate those works into English, but otherwise the phrase meant absolutely nothing to me, so I went along to have a look. The footpaths were crowded with onlookers and eventually the solemn procession made its way along the street. I had never before seen copes, mitres, chasubles and similar exotic ecclesiastical apparel, nor had I ever smelt the faintest whiff of incense. I stood there in gaping wonder and suddenly became aware that the multitudes had vanished. I looked around, and there they were, all on their knees, rosary beads clicking loudly, murmuring their prayers. I was the only one still standing. Then I began to hear furious whispers. "Look at him", "Who's that?", "Must be a bloody Protestant" and so forth. This was clearly no place to be seen, dead or alive, and I tiptoed quickly away. The first of those alternatives seemed to be a distinct probability at that moment.

It was a strange, bewildering, sometimes frightening and very much a *foreign* world to be in. Although we in the North had been brought up to respect our Church and its clergy, this was something altogether different. Here was power such as I had never experienced it before. I was a complete outsider in a world to which I could never belong. It was equally obvious from public pronouncements (not least John Charles's famous Lenten Pastorals and his annual assault on Trinity College) that I wasn't particularly wanted anyway and didn't count at all in the divine scheme of things.

Many years later, I returned to the Republic as rector of Blackrock in Cork. As a more public figure, one was inevitably thrown into much closer contact with the Roman Catholic Church than ever before. I expected that the same atmosphere of ecclesiastical control and exclusion still prevailed, but it soon became clear that things had changed. Cornelius Lucey, a man with a fearsome reputation as an arch-conservative, who governed with a rod of iron, was bishop of the Diocese of Cork. I was very surprised to find him a most gracious and charming man who made even a junior Church of Ireland clergyman feel that he actually mattered, and that his opinions were taken seriously. I soon learned that he had a highly developed social conscience, had a very generous pastoral heart and was a man of profound personal humility.

Personal friendships with priests, religious and laity developed over the years and in my own pilgrimage I became deeply indebted to many of them for their friendship, support and growth in faith. Ordinary human decency, coupled with genuine sanctity, is a formidable and humbling combination. Side by side with this personal enrichment, there dawned recognition that one's fellow-pilgrims belonged to a Church that no longer had the awe-inspiring power it once had and was frequently on the defensive against its own members. The old "us and them" changed into a common recognition that we are in the same boat, struggling to convey a faith that made sense against a growing tide of scepticism and even outright hostility aimed at institutional religion in all its manifestations. A few months ago, at the height of a particularly ferocious media assault on the shortcomings of the Roman Catholic Church, Bishop Donal Murray said to me, "It must be great to be a Church of Ireland bishop at the moment." Well, it is, actually, but perhaps not exactly in the sense he intended. It is exhilarating and terrifying, rewarding and frustrating, but beneath it is a deep sense of partnership, across the board, that I never imagined would happen, an experience for which I am greatly privileged and profoundly thankful.

Rev Katherine Meyer

Katherine P. Meyer was born and grew up in the United States, and if you go back far enough, she is of German and Dutch ancestry. She has lived in Ireland for 18 years, part of that time in Northern Ireland and part in the Republic. She now holds both Irish and American citizenship. She has worked with the Corrymeela community and has served in Presbyterian congregations, both in Belfast and in Dublin. At present, she is the Presbyterian and Methodist chaplain in Trinity College Dublin, where she works as part of an ecumenical team alongside both Anglican and Roman Catholic colleagues.

During the late twentieth and early twenty-first centuries, immigration into Ireland has been increasing significantly, and I am one of the arrivals of the last decade. An Irish citizen with no Irish ancestry and a Presbyterian with no Scottish ancestry, I am now a small part of the changing face of Ireland and, perhaps, of the Presbyterian Church in Ireland.

I begin by stressing these aspects of my identity not because they make my story any more important than anyone else's, but simply to be honest about the fact that I cannot contribute to these "untold stories" on the basis of a rich Irish Protestant past or of long Irish Protestant memories.

However, what I hope I *can* do is to highlight what I have come to believe is one of the defining characteristics of being a Christian in the Reformed tradition in the Republic of Ireland today. It is this: that we know something about belonging to both minority and majority communities at the same time. And I suspect that this multiple belonging has a number of rich and potentially fruitful implications, many of which have yet to be fully explored.

Let me explain what I mean. To be a Presbyterian in the Republic of Ireland is to be part of a small minority community. In all kinds of interesting and complex ways, we know something of what being a minority in this way can be like and can do to a community.

There are the obvious things, the frequent invisibility, the general ignorance, and of course, the humour. I once explained to a woman I had just met that I was an ordained Presbyterian minister, only to hear her introduce me, a few minutes later, as "Sister Katherine, who belongs to the Presbyterian order".

How you relate to the wider community, and how the wider community perceives you, are always going to be issues for a minority of any kind. Having said that, however, the more important issues are arguably going to be those which have to do with our own *self*-understanding.

So part of the experience of being in a minority community has to do with having to decide what really is most important to our identity, not as Christians (that is another question!) but as *Reformed* Christians. We ought to know only too well the importance of leaving room for dissenting voices within the wider Christian community to be heard. But those voices are inside us as well. Thus we may need to decide which is more important: belonging to a tradition in which differences are openly acknowledged and addressed in agreed and respectful ways; or belonging to a tradition which finds its cohesiveness not in a way of being together but in the exercise of a strict doctrinal conformity.

We also have to be more honest, I think, about how we relate to the present majority, Roman Catholic Christian tradition in Ireland. And here again we have a choice. There are those of us who seem to be so strangely lacking in confidence about our ability to negotiate difference in some kind of respectful, meaningful way that our only recourse is to deny significant difference and blame all disharmony on those whom we decide are not as broadminded as we are. We are sometimes given, and sometimes embrace, the label "ecumenical", but we are far from being ecumenical in any true sense.

There are also those of us, however, who bear a mirror image of this fear of difference. We are sometimes given, and sometimes embrace, the label "evangelical", but we are far from being evangelical in any true sense. Our fear of difference is seen in our wish to be increasingly non-denominational in our identity, precisely, it seems, because the historic denominations, in spite of their particular identifying characteristics, are nevertheless seedbeds of continuing and often troubling diversity. So those of us in this group choose to find our sense of ourselves in the repeated expression of a small number of unwavering theological positions.

All of us in these two groups are of course still participating in that terrible and familiar process of defining ourselves over against others, whoever those others may be. The great challenge we both face is whether or not we can find a way to embrace a Reformed identity which is *truly* ecumenical and *truly* evangelical, an identity which both opens to and risks knowing the other (both within the Presbyterian community and outside it), and is itself open to being transformed in ways we ourselves cannot yet imagine.

But finally, we need to remember that other dimension of our particular context, which is that we are also part of an overwhelming majority Christian community in this country. Thus, if we are honest, we as Presbyterians also know something of what being part of a majority can do to you, the easy assumptions and bland forms of generosity with which we too can be so quickly satisfied, and the unthinking ignorance of other minorities which we too can so readily display.

It is my hope that this "minority inside a majority" status which is also ours will make us more suited to one of the most central and defining tasks for the Christian Church in the twenty-first century, that of serious and committed participation in interfaith dialogue. This is because such conversations, whatever else they require, often ask of their participants a seemingly impossible combination of vulnerability and openness on the one hand, and confident and passionate conviction on the other, and these can seem almost impossible to combine. But to the extent that Reformed Christians in Ireland can embrace with dignity both our majority and our minority contexts, along with the uncomfortable truths inherent in each, we may find ourselves able to enter into such conversations with admirable commitment, self-awareness and hope.

Robert Myerscough

Robert Myerscough was born and educated in Dublin. He was Managing Director and Deputy Chairman of Coyle Hamilton Ltd. until he resigned in 1988 to pursue personal interests. He has been associated with Music in Great Irish Houses from its early days and now serves as its president. He was also a founder of Cothú, now Business to the Arts. An avid gardener, he attended a course in garden design at the Royal Botanic Gardens in Kew in 1990 and practised as a garden designer for the next ten years. Married with one son, he lives in County Wicklow.

Mixed Blessings

I was fortunate to be born in Dublin, into a Protestant family that had become prosperous in the first half of the twentieth century. This prosperity was almost entirely due to the business acumen of my grandfather, Frederick S. Myerscough. He would not have had this opportunity if his father had not come here from Lancashire to take up a teaching appointment just before 1900. Samuel S. Myerscough had become a convert to Roman Catholicism, as had two of my grandfather's siblings.

By 1922, Fred, as he was known, had already founded the first firm of insurance brokers in Ireland; Coyle & Company was named after his business partner Alfred Coyle. My father and I spent our careers in this company, later to become the Coyle Hamilton Group. That same year saw the formation of Goff's Bloodstock Sales as a limited liability company with Fred S. Myerscough as one of the founding directors. In 1925, he was able to get control of the business, and remained its chairman up to his death. Goff's would be served by two further generations, right up to the end of the last century.

The two businesses, insurance and bloodstock sales, expanded and grew despite the tough economic conditions confronting the fledgling Irish State in the 1920s. The following years, in the aftermath of the Wall Street crash and the Emergency, presented conditions in which only the fittest survived. Despite these challenges, Fred had also become a significant and successful racehorse owner, and ultimately owner-trainer at his home in Sandyford, sending out "The Phoenix" to win both the Irish 2000 Guineas and Derby in 1943, following which he became one of the first stallions to be syndicated.

My father, Cyril F. Myerscough, received his education, first at Earlsfort House Preparatory School, where Samuel Beckett was also a pupil. Dad always said that his only academic distinction was in being at school with Beckett! From there he went to public school in England and to Trinity College, Dublin.

My father married an Englishwoman, a tennis star who came to play at the annual Fitzwilliam Championships, and a fellow Anglican, but his two sisters married Catholics. The elder's husband was a Trinity-educated British Army doctor with liberal views, but their two daughters married English and Dutch husbands, both of whom were from Protestant traditions, reversing the denominations of their parents' marriage. The younger sister married a lawyer, whose upbringing in County Cork had been more traditional.

My great-aunt Alice, who was a devout Catholic, hero-worshipped her two brothers, one of whom was my grandfather. The other, the eldest of the family, had been sent to Stoneyhurst College, the well-known Catholic public school, which led to his becoming a Jesuit priest. Even at eight, I thought it odd that, when it came to my younger brother's christening, Alice stood outside, as her Church required. I probably did not question religious differences to any extent, so possibly it was because my parents were affronted.

Prior to my grandfather's death, we lived in Kilmacud Road, Dundrum. This was a very Protestant road in a large Church of Ireland parish. Most of our near neighbours were of the same persuasion. We lived on the edge of the countryside in those days. The only instance of religious friction that I can recall in my life was when we were "invaded" by an opposing gang of equally small Catholic children from the village. I don't recall what provoked this incident in an otherwise peaceful neighbourhood.

However, my sister and I were conscious of differences between Catholics and us, even at a young age, probably because my mother had to provide fish on Fridays for her live-in maid. The chapel in Dundrum, as we referred to it, had not been extended at that stage. We were intrigued by what lay within its dark interior. Eventually we persuaded our maid to take us there. She allowed us to dip our hands in the holy water; the confessionals frightened us and we stood in awe at the sight of the candles and votive lights in front of all the statues. Following this, we purchased two little red-glassed votive lights for our playhouse in the garage!

Both my brother and I were educated at Castle Park preparatory school, which had been founded to prepare boys for English public schools, and in 1949 it was still very much of that ethos. We then went on to St Columba's College.

My wife is an Anglican, and our son was baptised into the Church of Ireland. My sister married a Norwegian, and their two daughters were educated in Norway as well as at Newtown School, Waterford.

Maintaining the tradition of inter-denominational marriages in the family, my younger brother Philip married a Catholic girl, but on the occasion of their marriage, there was recognition of our family's tradition when Dean Victor Griffin and a detachment of the choir of St Patrick's Cathedral were asked to participate. (My father was a lay member of the Board of the Cathedral at that time, a role he played for some 15 years. I also served the cathedral for a similar time and was married there.) Naturally, as required in mixed marriages, Philip and Jane's four children have been confirmed as Catholics, but each has received part of their education at St Columba's College in Rathfarnham, the second generation to do so.

My great-grandfather was obviously a man of deep religious conviction. His children were equally committed, whether Roman Catholic or Anglican. Both my parents were regular churchgoers and brought us up in the same way, and our cousins also had a Christian upbringing. I do not know whether it is the mixing and re-mixing of denominations that has diluted adherence to either side in the fifth generation, or the very mixed messages we all receive through the media. Perhaps these are both reasons why the latest generation of our family finds little to attract them to formal religion. No doubt our forbears would look at this askance, but then the world has changed immeasurably in the last 80 years.

Archbishop John Neill

His Grace the Most Reverend John R.W. Neill was elected Church of Ireland Archbishop of Dublin in August 2002. He has served in the Church of Ireland for 33 years, over half of that time as a bishop, in the west and in the south-east, before his appointment as Archbishop. He has been deeply involved in ecumenical work, serving both as President of the Council of Churches for Britain and Ireland and as a member of the Central Committee of the World Council of Churches. He is married to Betty, and they have three grown-up sons all living and working in Ireland.

A Bishop's Story

Four incidents stand out in my memory illustrating something of what it is to belong to the minority Protestant community. They span a period of 50 years. I grew up in a rectory. There was usually a girl who worked for my mother in the home. Often these girls belonged to the Roman Catholic Church, and my mother and grandmother were not reticent in telling them the errors of their Church! I remember asking, as small boys do, the most awkward of questions: "Mum, how do we know we are right and they are wrong?" The answer stays with me to this day: "John, do you not believe in God?" My memory must be flawed, and the judgement a bit harsh, but it reflects something of the inner confidence and certainty within a part of a minority in the Ireland of the early 1950s. There was a sense of isolation, but we did not feel under threat. My paternal grandparents had left Cork for London 30 years earlier following the setting up of the Free State. Despite an English education, my father, as the youngest of a large family, could not wait to return, and did so shortly before his ordination. His identification with things Irish was total.

The second incident happened about 30 years ago when I was a young rector in west Cork. My wife and I were friendly with the local Mercy Sisters. Talking late into the night in our rectory, we would tell stories of the way we perceived each other. I recounted some of the stories told to me in that parish that represented something of the fear and suspicion still alive in the Church of Ireland community. These stories related to pressures on "mixed" marriages, the taking over of Protestant businesses and the loss of Protestant farms. In all these stories, the Legion of Mary played a role, however mythical that was! Then one of the nuns told almost identical stories which were alive and well in the community. The difference in our respective tales was that, in her case, the sectarian agent was the Masonic Order. These stories portrayed communities in isolation one from the other. They reflected greater fear than I had ever experienced growing up, but which I was quickly to learn about in rural Ireland where I have spent most of my ministry.

The other incidents relate to my time as a bishop in the West of Ireland, perhaps some 15 years ago. Each occurred as I introduced a new rector to a parish, and took place during the speeches at the social gathering following the liturgical celebration. The first was in a town with a very good ecumenical spirit, and the choir of the local Roman Catholic parish led the liturgy. I spoke of the marvellous manner in which the "two communities" pulled together in that area. The next speaker, a civic dignitary, gently chided me for speaking of two communities — he only knew of one. I was struck that evening by the fact that people there were ready to see themselves as one community with a rich diversity rather than as two communities living side by side.

Soon after, in another town not too far away, I introduced a new clergyman. The chairperson of the local urban council welcomed the rector to the town "on behalf of the Catholic community". This reflected the feeling that the Church of Ireland was somehow alien to the "real" community that was Roman Catholic. It was hardly a coincidence that another local politician always made my single surname into a double-barrelled name, linking it with one of my forenames, and he managed to do the same for two of my predecessors, all of whom had straightforward surnames! We were categorised as a class apart, part of the old ascendancy! The perceptions behind these incidents relate to attitudes within the Protestant community as much as beyond it.

Perception is important for the self-understanding of a minority and also for the way that it is valued in society. In terms of self-understanding, issues of fear and self-confidence arise. For the sake of its role in Ireland, it has to be teased out whether Protestantism represents a welcome diversity within the community, however appreciated that adjunct may be.

Ecumenism has allowed a self-confidence to mature among Protestants that is positive rather than negative. My earliest experiences of confidence may have been negative, but there was little room for fear. Fear has been the most damaging aspect of the minority. It has involved keeping "a low profile" and maintaining a distance. Fear may be based on both mythology and fact, but it is fomented through isolation and lack of self-confidence. Protestants, particularly from small rural communities, who have ventured out of the constraints of a tightly knit circle, have found that not only is their contribution welcomed, but that they grow in their own appreciation of their own tradition.

The role of a minority tradition within the Republic of Ireland is also deeply affected by factors external to that tradition. The issue of whether the Church of Ireland represents a diversity within modern Irish society or whether it is an adjunct to that society is relevant far beyond these western towns in which I discovered those contrasting attitudes. These attitudes are mirrored in the relations between the Churches, the first being positively ecumenical, the second negatively sectarian. This impinges on how Irish society defines itself, either as richly diverse, or as monolithic in culture, religion and ethos. Pluralism is not to be feared. The Church of Ireland is in a position to make a serious contribution to political and social debate, reflecting diversity even within Christian perspectives — an opportunity that it has not always grasped.

Warren Nelson

Warren David Nelson was born in Belfast in 1938 to a Northern mother and southern father. He grew up in Drogheda, County Louth and was educated at Drogheda Grammar School. He spent seven years in the textile industry before studying at TCD and being ordained in the Church of Ireland. He was a curate on the Shankill Rd and a rector in Counties Tipperary and Cavan, but most of his ministry was as a lecturer in the Irish Bible School, Coalbrook, Thurles. He now lives in active retirement near Tullamore, County Offaly, still teaches and enjoys DIY.

A Man of the Cloth

When I moved to Tullamore, I had to get myself a dentist. He looked at my name, "You're not Irish are you?" Well, Michael is Jewish, Patrick is Roman, Peter is Greek, so who is Irish anyway? But it was nothing new for me, many would not consider me Irish despite having origins in Meath going back hundreds of years, possibly originating from the O'Neills. To be Irish, the popular synonym asserts, is to be Catholic; that is, strictly speaking, *Roman* Catholic. Yet I am an Irish patriot, I love my country and all her people . . . without having to hate any other. I am proud of our flag . . . except when I see it being used as a party political badge. I would like to see the language flourish . . . but get vexed when it is pumped up with the steroids of compulsion and used as a talisman of nationalistic orthodoxy. I vote, I pay my taxes, care for our environment and have worn the harp briefly in the Civil Defence. Must I change my name or religion to be Irish?

As I grew up, the symbiotic relationship between the Catholic Church and the State was at its zenith. I dreaded the Corpus

Christi processions of the 1940s and 1950s, I have never liked the emphasis on Sunday sport and I still believe that the *Ne Temere* decree which led to the decimation of a minority community was wrong. Is this why I am not really Irish?

I worked on looms weaving traditional linen damask as a young man. Some years later, having been a migrant in Australia, and having come under Christian conviction, I studied and became a Church of Ireland minister, but not in any professional sense; I am strictly an amateur. What I believe, rather than holding any particular office, makes the essential me. Once I found myself in a kitchen on the pre-Troubles, pre-redevelopment Shankill Road. As a green curate, I cast around for some point of commonality. I spied a framed City and Guilds Final Certificate in Linen Weaving on the wall belonging to Billy, son of the house. Here was my contact. "I have one of those," I hastily said. "Well, fancy", said Billy's mother, "a man of your cloth havin' one o' tham." I am a man of the cloth.

Were I to see a protest march behind the banner "DOWN with RELIGION", I would join in *provided* I could state that by "religion" I mean the unthinking, encultured, ritualistic thing that passes for Christianity in Ireland, Protestant and Catholic alike. Two radical truths from the Bible have been forgotten, skewed, jettisoned or buried. The first is that human nature is thoroughly sinful, without exception, and needs to be remade. Human nature is admired in the arts, flattered in politics and media, excused in the courts, pandered to by intellectuals and pampered by advertisers with the result that problems of society multiply beyond the control of the experts. The great postmodern fallacy is that you can have a morality without need of convictions, now and hereafter . . . we do not, we cannot, earn it. Far too much Irish religion, like its secular cousins, flatters human nature by letting us think that we can put God in our debt by our giving, our decency, our ceremonies, or our piety. Whereas, in fact, our salvation is based only on Christ's atoning work on the Cross, and *is* ours to have, to enjoy and to live out, by faith: that is to say, by trusting God that it is, indeed, now ours. What! Without our goodness? Well, if your "goodness" is only practised to earn your salvation, it's not goodness, is it? Is this being presumptuous? No, it is honouring God by taking him at his word. Presumption is imagining that you can earn your passage to Heaven. Yet an alien eavesdropper at any Irish funeral would come away with that very conclusion. These convictions of mine, if they must be labelled, are best described as "Evangelical", which is why I seldom use the word "Protestant". Indeed, for all the baggage it has picked up, I could happily see that word disappear.

When I had worked five years in parishes, North and south, I left the regular ministry and gave 20 years to Bible teaching in a quiet corner on the Kilkenny/Tipperary border. With others from backgrounds in most denominations, we endeavoured to teach all comers to think biblically. The missing dimension in Irish life is the willingness to let the Bible, interpreted by all the good standards of literary analysis, speak for itself, and to speak into all areas of economics, health, culture, politics *and* religion. It needs to be heard, not muffled by 2,000 years of religious tradition, free from sectarian prejudice, denominational strife, liberal waffling, fundamentalist ranting or condescending intellectualism, and certainly not in Shakespearian English. Or to tumble the argument into another arena, would that the biblical diagnosis of life got a fraction of the attention, glossy paper and electronic imagery given to the foul-mouthed, the morally confused, the overpaid and the hedonistically self-centred. What an Ireland we would have then, land of saints and scholars.

Strangely enough, the Republic has become more Protestant, if we must use the word. Often we are indeed, literally, singing from the same hymn sheet. But people have behaved as they would at the pick 'n' mix counter of their supermarket, and form the Protestant fixtures they have chosen: Questioning of Authority, Private Judgement and Freedom of Conscience. But these should be part of a balanced selection, along with: the Authority of Scripture, Justification by Faith, the Call to Holiness of Living, Evangelism and Missionary Concern; not to be sold separately.

Yes, the dentist also told me to open my mouth.

Senator David Norris

David Norris is a member of Seanad Éireann, a conservationist and a Joycean scholar. He was a Senior Lecturer in the English Department at Trinity College Dublin from 1968–94. He has broadcast and published internationally on a variety of literary, sociological and legal topics, and has lectured at international scholarly gatherings in Europe, the Middle East and North America.

Growing up, I was never greatly troubled by being a Protestant; it was far more problematic being a poof. In fact, I didn't even know I was perceived as a Protestant until a group of school pals and myself received the military attention of some kids from CUS as we waited for the bus to take us up to the cricket field in Stillorgan. They hooted the word "Prodissen" at us and challenged us to admit that we didn't believe in the Virgin Mary. This I refused to do.

Indeed, most of my childhood friends outside school were Roman Catholics. It did occasionally lead to a sectarian jibe of one sort or another. I recall one memorable day when my oldest and best friend and I had a disagreement about who should take charge of a dinky car in the sandpit. We traded insults and his final dig was, "Ya, you're not even a Catholic." I went home in floods of tears to my mother. When she inquired what was wrong, I told her that my friend said I wasn't a Catholic. "Of course you are darling, don't you say it every Sunday in the creed, 'I believe in one Holy Catholic and Apostolic Church'. You are just not part of the Roman error like Michael." I didn't quite know what the Roman error was but I knew I now had in my possession the debating equivalent of an intercontinental ballistic missile. I couldn't wait to share the glad tidings with my pal who of course repeated it to his parents. The result did not lead to a strengthening of ecumenism in Dublin 4!

Most of my friends went to the Star of the Sea Church in Sandymount for mass and confession. These were sacraments for which I longed. I delighted in the sound of Latin and the smell of incense. I ached to go to confession to a nice young priest but such delights were forbidden to infant members of the C of I.

Nonetheless, there was a certain variety of worship available even to us separated brethren. When we were feeling Low Church, we went to St Mary's in Donnybrook but if we pined for a bit more ceremonial, we attended St Bartholomew's Church in Clyde Road which was as high as hell and actually had incense and optional confession as well as the occasional sung Mass in Latin.

Infected with the religious enthusiasm of my grandmother and my mother, both of whom enjoyed going to church, I found I quite relished the services. There was, however, the occasional disappointment. When I was being confirmed I had visions in my mind of the stained glass window in the church which showed the Holy Ghost descending on the head of Christ when he was baptised in the Jordan by John the Baptist. I fully expected some kind of electrical thrill to pass through my body as the Archbishop laid his hands upon my head. I knelt there waiting for something that never happened until one of my companions gave me a sharp kick in the ankle and told me to get up out of that.

Of course, there were serious aspects to religious division. I vaguely remember the scandal caused by the boycott at Fethard-on-Sea. The bigotry of course was not all on one side. I had a nice old great-aunt, my mother's aunt, who lived in what had been a lovely rambling old house in the country. From all her pregnancies, only one child survived and he was naturally or perhaps unnaturally cosseted by his mother. He got it into his head that if he married a Roman Catholic he would be disinherited. I am sorry to say that this could well have been true in the 1950s. When she got pneumonia, the local nurse was called in to look after her. The nurse struck up a friendship with the son of the house, which eventually led to a secret Catholic marriage. The lonely young man used to leave his even lonelier mother alone in the house at night while he went to visit his secret family. When she eventually died, he turned up accompanied by his children, which gave a satisfactorily physical confirmation of his matrimonial position. These kids would be my second cousins and yet I am sorry and ashamed to say that since that day over 40 years ago I have not seen sight or sound of one of them.

Of course, in extenuation it must be said that these were the days of the *Ne Temere* decree. As a result of this unjust ruling from Rome if a member of the One True Church married a member of the C of I, the heathen partner had to sign away all his or her rights in the religious education of the children. This led to the wiping out of the vulnerable Anglican minority in many rural parishes.

The principal differences that I recall between myself and my Roman Catholic friends was the fact that we were encouraged to study the Bible. In Church on Sundays, just before the sermon, the children were led out into the vestry for Bible lessons. We each had little stamp albums and every Sunday our attendance was rewarded by a brightly coloured stamp depicting some incident from the Gospel, which we duly stuck into the album. When it was full, it could be sent to London and in return a copy of the New Testament would be sent back as a prize. My grandmother and my mother both told me Bible stories before I went to sleep and my mother gave me a book of such stories when I first went to boarding school, which was my only comfort as I was not permitted to take my teddy bear with me to school.

Nowadays, of course, the relationships between the Churches are much happier and it has become evident that the Anglican Church (the Church of Ireland) in particular is very close indeed to Rome in essentials of belief and ritual.

This is not entirely positive, because the translation of the Roman missal and the Cranmer Prayer Book into modern English have led us not to the heights of religious ecstasy but to a plateau of vulgar banality. In particular, we seem to have caught the general infection of that horrible and intrusive Sign of Peace which we are instructed from the altar to make with our neighbours at communion. This is in my opinion an insincere gesture in most cases and the liturgical equivalent of lapdancing. However, perhaps it is a small price to pay for improved relations between the Churches and as it usually occurs just before the offertory, one can avoid the nastiness of contact by pretending to fumble in one's pocket for the collection.

Caoimhghín Ó Caoláin TD

Caoimhghín Ó Caoláin has been the Sinn Féin TD for Cavan/Monaghan since 1997. Following the 2002 general election he became the leader in the Dáil of the five Sinn Féin TDs. He has played a central role in his party's peace strategy and was involved in the negotiations leading to the Good Friday Agreement.

A Border Signpost to a Better Ireland

My native Monaghan is a truly diverse county and is home to communities of all the main religious denominations in Ireland. While the majority of its population are Catholic, the Protestant Churches are strongly represented. There are many congregations of the Church of Ireland, the Presbyterian and Methodist Churches. The Elim Pentecostal Church, which is the largest of the other Protestant denominations, was founded in Monaghan. The Free Presbyterian Church also has a congregation in our county. County Cavan, which I represent in the Dáil with County Monaghan, has a very significant Protestant minority.

I was brought up a Catholic in Monaghan town and from my earliest childhood I have enjoyed the friendship of others of my own age of various religious denominations. This was not regarded as anything extraordinary. Difference was of course recognised in terms of education and churchgoing but by and large there was integration on a social and economic level. We knew diversity before the modern meaning of the term evolved.

I am glad to say that those friendships have endured over the years. They were often difficult years but I am pleased and proud

to record that while there may have been different political perspectives, those views never soured our relationships. As an
elected representative, I am called upon regularly to assist con-
stituents of all religious denominations and political persuasions.
I have worked with individual members of minority faiths as well
as ministers and congregations. That is an ongoing responsibility
for me as a TD and councillor and one I am very proud to fulfil.

It is a notable fact that, despite our proximity to the counties in
which the conflict of much of the past 30 years raged so intensely
and so tragically, community relationships remained strong in
County Monaghan and sectarianism was never allowed to take
root. People of different religious and political persuasions, including republicans, played their part in ensuring that the noxious
weed of inter-community strife never flourished in our county.

That is not to say that the conflict did not deeply affect County
Monaghan. Combatants on all sides — republicans, the British
army, loyalists — inflicted death and injury. Much pain was endured by both civilians and combatants and the legacy remains.
But perhaps in Monaghan we are better placed than most to deal
with that legacy as we build new and stronger relationships on
this island which we share.

Here, the foundations for such bridge-building are deeper.
People of the various religious faiths have built strong inter-
denominational relationships. These have enriched the lives of
everyone, strengthened our community and given each of us an
understanding and a willingness to confront the ugliness and total
unacceptability of sectarianism wherever it rears its ugly head.
That experience is needed now more than ever.

Just as we cannot separate County Monaghan from events
across the partition boundary, neither can we neglect the context
of the 26-county State in which we live. For me, pluralism has always been more than a theory. It was a scandal that, for decades,
the teachings of the Catholic Church were allowed to dominate
the law in this State, especially with regard to issues like divorce
and contraception. That represented real discrimination against
citizens — both Catholic and non-Catholic — who did not accept

those teachings and who were denied the freedom to act according to their conscience. My own experience in a very mixed community, as well as my republican belief in civil rights, led me and my party, Sinn Féin, to support the long overdue ending of those unjust laws and progress towards a pluralist State. Much progress has been made, due in no small way to the constructive role played by political representatives drawn from minority faith communities.

I believe the best guarantors of the rights of any group of citizens are those citizens themselves. By actively participating in the civic life of society, they are best placed to ensure that their rights are vindicated. I believe this truth is becoming increasingly clear to sections of the minority community on this island. Their best interests are surely served in an all-Ireland context where they can exercise much more influence as citizens rather than as disconnected subjects in an increasingly disunited kingdom. I know that many in the Protestant community in the 26 counties would agree with that.

It is very important to record that there were and are many people who challenge the perceived "norm" that places all Catholics and all Protestants in ready-made political boxes. Both in my home county and beyond, I have been very conscious of the significant contribution to Irish republicanism made by people from a Protestant background, both in the past and in contemporary Ireland. There is a spectrum of political opinion within the Protestant community as much as in the Catholic. For obvious reasons, the republican end of the spectrum within the Protestant tradition has not always been the most visible. But it is very much there.

For too long power without accountability was wielded by elites in the main Churches and by denominational politicians in both States on this island. Thankfully, those days are over.

Whether or not you are a member of an organised religion, you will agree that much constructive work is done by people of all faiths in the service of their own communities and of the wider community. Many of them are motivated by a real community and civic spirit. Sadly, this sense of social responsibility is on the wane in broad sections of Irish society. Individualism, consumerism and gross materialism are dominant in our "mé féin" economy. The sense of responsibility to others, especially those who are marginalised and discriminated against, is shared by nearly all religions, both Christian and non-Christian. That surely can be built upon.

I believe this spirit *is* being built upon in my native County Monaghan. It is far from perfect but we have developed a diverse and pluralist community, one which, I firmly believe, is a microcosm of the better Ireland to which we all aspire.

Risteárd Ó Glaisne

Risteárd Ó Glaisne was born in West Cork in 1927 and was educated at the Bandon Grammar School and Trinity College Dublin. He taught in Dublin secondary schools for over 30 years. He has been a freelance journalist and broadcaster and is the author of 27 published books. He has travelled widely in Western Europe.

Our parents married comparatively late but were very much in love and took to family life in a very natural way. They had four children — three boys and a girl, in that order. We grew up on a farm three miles north of Bandon. Both Mum and Dad were of farming background. Since the seventeenth century, Protestants have been established in West Cork and my family seem to have been there for all that time.

Most Protestants were relatively better off than their Roman Catholic neighbours. The emergence of the new Irish State was not something they had asked for, because, as elsewhere in Ireland, there had been a symbiotic relationship between almost all Protestants and the British government in Ireland. However, the situation had now changed and Protestants who remained in the 26-county State realised that they would have to adjust to some degree at least under the new order.

The practical attitude of many Protestants in West Cork during the War of Independence and the Civil War had been apolitical and the next generation was in many ways reared to that attitude too. Nonetheless, we were told by our religious leaders that it was our Christian duty to vote in elections and that had important implications. Dad made common cause with neighbours on certain public issues. Politics were involved there, directly or indirectly — mostly indirectly in Dad's case.

We used to go the Methodist church. Our religion was simple but basic, founded hugely on the Bible, particularly the New Testament, where Christ's emphasis on love of God and neighbour was so very apparent and challenging.

Christ called for personal commitment. This was fully accepted within Methodism as essential to Christian spirituality and behaviour. As I moved into my teens, however, I noted that within the Christian community — Methodism or otherwise — a great gap yawned between theory and practice. I became disillusioned about professedly Christian institutions or individuals seeking power in any of its many forms — psychological, political, financial, etc. I still remain unimpressed by much so-called Christianity. In fact, when trying to be starkly objective, the deeper my faith in Christ, the less I admire many Christians. I do not of course assume myself personally to be free of responsibility and guilt here, and I take it that our shared guilt goes far to explain why so many people are willingly strangers to the palpable benefits which even the most modest of Christians can still know and love. I have, however, long believed that people who abandon the Church rather than stay within it in order to help reform it are guilty of a dishonesty far more grievous than any to be seen in those who take too lightly the grave responsibilities of belonging to the Church.

When I speak of the Church, I mean those who have intended to take commitment to Christ seriously. Those concerned with our upbringing did not encourage us to set ourselves up in judgement upon the doctrines of others who were not Methodists or Protestants of some other sort. We did, however, come to know the differences between us gradually and certain things in Roman Catholic doctrine are to me unacceptable, but I never had any reason to doubt that religion had a benign influence upon the Christian people around me, most of who were Roman Catholics.

In school, Irish history interested me, especially that relating to the last couple of hundred years. I was surprised at first to find that certain Protestants — Wolfe Tone, Robert Emmet, Thomas Davis, Douglas Hyde and so on — had been leaders of thought and action in the life of the nation. Early in my teens I read Terence MacSwiney's *Principles of Freedom* and Patrick Pearse's *Story of a Success* with Desmond Ryan's biography *The Man Called Pearse*. These led me to consider the nature of Irish nationalism. Some of Pearse's views or metaphors seemed to me so unhealthy as to be almost blasphemous, yet I found very much in him to like too. Both MacSwiney and he conveyed very strikingly the creative potential of a wise nationalism — and the substantially destructive effects of British (or any other) imperialism. I began to see that Irish Protestant involvement in imperialist ambitions had damaged our Christian witness. Violence of any sort and from any quarter I abhor and mostly condemn; on the other hand — so far anyway — I very sadly accept that there are situations where undue force has to be met by some measure of violence. I have no reason to suppose that Hitler or agents of the British Empire (or other military and economic amalgamations) would voluntarily confer a proper freedom on vulnerable populations. I know that fear and violence breed fear and violence: I am grateful for having had a life almost wholly free of either. I feel strongly about fomenting fear or violence. Such fomentation is all too common.

All modern nations should, I believe, be seen as pluralist — enjoying and cultivating valuable traditions but not by any means incapable of a discerning will to change, or to welcome others and something of their ways of life. However, there is such a thing as chequebook imperialism and a natural continuity is as desirable in a nation as in an individual: that needs to be remembered. Evidence of a distinctive Irish nationhood still operative in our current society takes us back well over 2,000 years. The Gaelic, Celtic, element in our culture is still strong and the Irish language is its most powerful and meaningful vehicle. I was most fortunate in acquiring a fluent and loving familiarity with Irish before I was 20, living with native Irish speakers and giving Irish a primacy in my life which many speakers of English would find hard to credit. Most of the books I have written are in Irish and they reflect the thinking of a contemporary Irishman and Protestant on a variety of themes — religion, literature, politics, travel, women's liberation, education, radio, geopolitical matters and so on. I use Irish rather than English for most of my writings because I am convinced that unless those of us who are qualified to use it do so whenever possible, it will die. In terms of national continuity, that could be seen objectively only as a tragic loss and a proof of almost criminal negligence. There is nothing astonishing about knowing Irish as well as English. In my personal formation, both Irish and English have illumined my life. One of my books, *To Irish Protestants*, is in English and it not only shows in me a sturdy Protestantism but also a strongly ecumenical streak, for Christ wanted His followers to be one.

I have enjoyed my life in Ireland amongst my fellow-countrywomen and -men. I have also enjoyed the company of people in and from many other countries. I feel enriched by them all.

God has been good and most of the people I have known have been very good to me too.

Olivia O'Leary

Olivia O'Leary has presented television and radio programmes for the last three decades for both RTE and the British Channels, BBC and ITV. As a print journalist, she has written about politics for both The Irish Times *and* The Sunday Tribune. *She is the presenter of the BBC Radio 4 programme* Between Ourselves, *which won a Sony Award three years ago and was nominated again last year. In Ireland, she has had her own discussion programme,* Later with O'Leary *on RTE television and has an interview series,* In My Life, *on RTE radio. With Dr Helen Burke, she has co-written the authorised biography of former Irish President, Mary Robinson. Born in Borris, County Carlow in 1949, she is married with one daughter.*

Protestant Tea

She was probably my mother's closest friend and she loved my mother in the same way I did. That made her family. So when I write about my Aunty Betty Young, I'm not writing about Irish Protestants as a separate group. I'm writing about someone who was an essential part of our lives.

There were differences, most of them pointed up gaily by Betty herself. Protestants went to church at a reasonable hour, like noon, so by the time the Youngs called to our house for a post-service cup of tea, all our Catholic friends were leaving. She would have none of our strong-as-your-arm brew but would be made a delicate infusion, the sort which allowed you to see the bottom of the cup. "Is that Protestant tea?" she'd check, before she drew out her Silk Cut.

The differences, of course, went deeper. My mother had eight children. Betty had three and regarded my mother as too much a slave to all of us. Without her actually saying so, we knew she disapproved of the price Catholic women paid for their large un-planned families. She would determinedly pull my mother out to play golf, to have a drink in the approved local lounge, to go to a concert in Carlow or Kilkenny. We knew whenever she came that Mum was going to be hauled away for recreation. One of my little sisters would start to cry as soon as Betty's light certain step was heard in the hallway. "Oh no, don't go away with Aunty Betty Young."

Betty had no patience with the Catholic Madonna syndrome. She constantly challenged my mother's attempts to be the ideal wife and mother — to sublimate her own needs to everyone else's. Betty was very Protestant in that way: she believed pas-sionately in individual freedom, most particularly her own. She always had her own car, a red Volkswagen, and she financed it by various sidelines: she supplied eggs to the local hatcheries; she acted as an agent for knitting machines; she ran her home, Lorum Rectory, as an Irish Country House. She kept up a constant and energetic battle for her own independence from her husband, "Bus" Young, the local Bank of Ireland manager who also farmed locally, as his family had done for generations. Betty's people, on the other hand, came from Northern Ireland. Betty graduated from Queen's and, before she married, taught in France and the UK and Ireland.

My mother and herself were intelligent women surviving in a small village. They were members of a book club; I still remember the green-covered books with Aunty Betty's bold writing on the outside. They were members of the local ecumenical movement. They disapproved of the rules that didn't allow Catholics to at-tend Protestant services. (In our diocese, that was a reserved sin — you had to get pardon from the bishop for it and I can remem-ber Catholics standing miserably outside at the funerals of their Protestant friends.) They hated the Catholic rule that didn't allow Betty to be godmother to my sister Elizabeth. But they were loyal to their separate traditions. They both believed that mixed marriages brought problems and that people were generally better to marry within their own faith.

They disagreed on matters of doctrine. Betty had boxers, as horrible a set of dogs as ever I laid my eyes on. When I was a child, they terrified me and I didn't believe any of her sharp assurances that they wouldn't touch me as long as I stayed calm. I didn't want to wait that long. Anyway, Betty and my mother had a doctrinal disagreement about the dogs. "I believe firmly, Mary, that my doggies will be in heaven with me," pronounced Betty. My mother laughed her light sceptical laugh. "But Betty, there is absolutely no Christian teaching which supports that view." I listened with horror. Any heaven which held Aunty Betty's dogs was no place for me.

They both loved dogs. Betty had her pedigree boxers and wolfhounds. My mother had a series of strays who had wangled themselves into her affections. They would consult one another about doggy sicknesses and injuries. Betty was no dog snob. When one of our mongrels fell ill, she brought him home and nursed him back to health. And when our house was finally sold and the last dog left without a home, he was taken out to Young's and spoiled along with all the fancier mutts — and that was doggy heaven on earth.

Betty and my mother were both horrified by what was happening in Northern Ireland and supported the civil rights movement. I'm sure they both voted the same way and it certainly wasn't republican. They both played the organ in their respective churches and would exchange experiences on a Sunday morning; my mother got on with the parish priest, a shy and gruff old countryman who confided in her his secret passion for classical music. Betty had a constant tussle of wills with the man she always referred to in Gothic capitals as The Dean.

At Harvest Festival time, my mother and I would sometimes go up to the little Protestant church in Borris House grounds and help Betty with the flowers. I liked the way we were all doing up the church as though for a party and I wondered why we Catholics, in our rural church, didn't also give thanks for the harvest. But I was shocked by the way the Youngs chatted and laughed in the church. Even though there was no consecrated host, no tabernacle, I tiptoed around and spoke in whispers. They thought I was bats. I tried to talk out loud but years of Catholic conditioning choked me. "God'll getcha", I was warned at school when I did something irreverent and I didn't want to take the chance that God's long arm would indeed stretch out and get me, even in a Protestant church.

The Youngs were our link with the land. Even though we lived in a country village, we were bakers, townspeople. At haymaking time, my mother would go out with Betty to bring tea to Bus and his neighbours in the fields. They'd stay out there for hours, drinking in the dusty golden light and the lengthening shadows as the haystacks grew.

And all those neighbours would turn up with us at Young's annual St Stephen's Night party. The food was magic: Betty's own spiced beef, her own chutney, her own soda bread, her own cheese and her wonderful lemon curd.

But the best thing of all about these parties was the freedom. Betty let me drink, which I wasn't allowed to do in my more careful Catholic home. In Young's, I mastered the sickly taste of gin and orange, after which no drink was a problem. Teenagers like me were expected to hold our own in conversation, to sing and play at the piano. Often on these nights, I'd meet some of the racier Protestant boys from County Kildare, with whom I would end up snogging in the upstairs rooms. Aunty Betty soon hunted us down. "Liv O'Leary," she'd call, "Get downstairs immediately — what will I say to your mother!" But she wasn't too cross and I knew she wasn't going to say anything to my mother. She didn't think that girls should be too protected. The more you knew about the world, she believed, the better you could handle it, and I was only too ready to learn.

Sometimes she was bossy. Once, when my mother was ill and I was trying to mind her, Betty took one look at her and disappeared to the phone. When she came back, she had booked her into a nursing home in Carlow where Mum could recover. It never struck me to feel miffed. I was just grateful.

After my mother's funeral, Betty stayed late in our house, serving drinks and food, talking to visitors, doing all the things we were too numb to do. I knew she was shattered, as we were, but she didn't cry — that wasn't her way. Instead, she was with us, as she always had been. In later years, we'd gravitate towards Betty when we missed our mother. Somehow, she understood.

She'd continue to call in to our house on the Main Street, leaving her trusty Volks parked at any odd angle to the road, just like a cowboy abandoning his horse. She thought it was a great joke that she'd become an Old Age Pensioner. "The AOP is here," she'd call down the hallway — "The Ancient Old Protestant".

Funny, now that she's gone, the image that most often comes back to me is not of the strong-willed woman she was but of the moment on Stephen's Night when she sang her party piece. Standing alone in front of the fireplace, she'd close her eyes and in her light voice deliver a song full of longing for where she came from and regret for what had happened there. "And the green hills of Antrim", she'd sing, "are calling me home."

It brought tears to my eyes then. It still does.

Una O'Higgins O'Malley

Una O'Higgins O'Malley has been active in the peace movement of the 1970s, 1980s and early 1990s. She was a founder member of the Glencree Centre for Reconciliation and also President of the Irish Association. In her memoirs, From Pardon and Protest, *she has written of her appreciation of her Protestant and former unionist neighbours during her formative years. She chaired a committee which organised the memorable celebration in St Patrick's Cathedral of the visit to Dublin of Pope John Paul II. Subsequently when received in private audience by the Pope, she strongly requested his assistance in erasing the belief that to be Irish is to be Catholic. A collection of her poems, under the title* The Terrible Beauty, *is currently being considered for publication.*

As a child born five years after the State was founded, it seemed to me that everyone who was not a (Roman) Catholic was a Protestant — the Quaker doctor who lived around the corner, Senator the Countess of Desart (who I think was Jewish), Presbyterian friends in Belfast — all were to me "Protestants", I suppose because they were not Catholics. Though I have no recollection of distinctions being made to me, I know there was a "them and us" feeling in my way of looking at things; it wasn't that I felt superior to Protestants, as the lines below will demonstrate (though my religion was of course "the true one") — it was just that we were different:

A Dublin Dancing Class in the 1930s

The Protestant girls wore lovely lacy stockings
their mothers knitted as they watched the class
but my bookish mum could scarcely hold a needle
and my Gran was into three-ply that wouldn't last.

The Protestant girls had dainty fuzzy hug-me's
in lavender or pink or palest blue,
their shining curls seemed never to look greasy
as my limp bob was sadly wont to do.

The Protestant girls had fathers who would drive them
on Sundays to the mountains or the sea;
they worked high up in banks or in big business
but mine by then was part of history

As you grow up the whole perspective changes
and few things matter like they used to do
but somehow I remember patterned stockings
and shining curls with smiling eyes of blue.

These things are never noted in the annals
where wars are listed each with its treaty,
only to some are they all that important
but for a time they meant a lot to me.

In my early years, my best friend and neighbour was Protestant
and it nearly broke my heart to think that she would go to hell
because she wasn't a Catholic. I tried to lure her into our church
for a visit, hoping that a sudden grace would hit her there and
that she would "turn"; when I eventually succeeded, what she
made of the purple shrouded statues in their Lenten coverings she
was too polite to say!

Before long, she went to Alexandra College, then in Earlsfort
Terrace, and I to the Sacred Heart Convent in Leeson Street. The
gardens of our two schools were back to back but apart from a
hockey match or two, the pupils never mixed. Once there was a
complaint from them that our tunics were so long the ball got
caught up in them but we were mindful of the admonitions of

Archbishop McQuaid on the subject of girl's dress, so we didn't shorten our skirts.

Later, the Protestants I knew best were mostly Anglo-Irish and former unionists. I have always felt that our neutrality in the Second World War cut us off from many of our own people as well as from our neighbours, resulting in an even stronger "them and us" outlook. The contribution of the Anglo-Irish and indeed of Irish Protestants to the arts, architecture, literature, music, medicine, horticulture, etc., is something the Republic has been very glad to build on but somehow not really to acknowledge. It seems to me that at the time the State was founded, a considerable effort was made to take into account this heritage and to acknowledge our debt to other than Catholic Ireland. The appointment of Senators such as W.B. Yeats, Sir John Keane, Lady Desart and Andrew Jameson broadened the outreach of the Oireachtas, while the first Constitution offered no special status to the Catholic Church. At a later stage, Liam Cosgrave, son of the first President of the Free State and himself by then Taoiseach, took a leaf out of his father's book by appointing Lord Iveagh to the Seanad. In all the recent celebrations for the State's acquisition of his home, Farmleigh, I was sad that I could not see mentioned that Benjamin Iveagh had served in the Seanad, something he considered a great honour. I know it is said that some of the early unionist senators contributed little to debates, but it was still a positive factor that they willingly agreed to take their seats as part of the ongoing nation.

After the assassination of my father in 1927 (when he was Vice-President and Minister for Justice), the messages of sympathy to my mother included many from Protestant Ministers and people who mourned his death and she was personally befriended with great kindness by some of the Senators mentioned above.

What remains now in this country of the proud Protestant heritage and witness? Sometimes I have met my childhood friend Norma, at the Poppy Day Remembrance Service at St Patrick's. At least, thanks mainly to the Good Friday Agreement, people can now emerge into the street afterwards without first furtively removing medals and decorations, as used to be the case in the past. On the whole, it is of course good that there should no longer be a "them and us" feeling, that we should no longer be surprised if Protestants do very well in Irish (as we used somehow be, in spite of the scholarship of Dubhglas de hÍde, Archbishop Donald Caird and other notable Protestant lovers of the Irish language). But I fear that we have mostly attained this mix by not duly respecting the diversity which preceded it, nor acknowledging much of our indebtedness to people who have kept things going in this country, which the rest of us would one day enjoy. Yes, I *have* heard about wicked and absentee landlords and I do know about many of our distresses; but the other side of the story is, I believe, not sufficiently respected and recorded.

Joe Patterson

Joe Patterson was born in Letterkenny, County Donegal on 1 November 1935. He was educated at Foyle College, Londonderry, Northern Ireland. He left college at 16 and went into the family businesses of butchering and farming. He was actively involved in the community of Letterkenny, but has lived in British Columbia, Canada, since 1974. He is married with three children, all born in County Donegal.

One Untold Story from County Donegal

I was born in Letterkenny in County Donegal, like many generations of my family before me. After college I went into the family business — butchering, farming, etc. I married in 1961 and we have three children. I was a founder member of the Letterkenny Chamber of Commerce, Assistant Director of the Letterkenny International Folk Festival for its first five years and was involved in many other voluntary community activities. Life went on.

In 1969, with the outbreak of violence in Northern Ireland and the IRA bombing campaign through the 1970s, business in the border towns in County Donegal experienced a boom. During this period, with the shoppers coming from Londonderry, only 20 miles away, having a contract with the Irish Army in Rockhill Barracks and an extra battalion of the Irish Army encamped outside the town, our business doubled.

However, things changed dramatically between September 1971 and June 1973, at which time we closed our doors for the last time. The events that led to this unhappy conclusion could be described, if one were to be charitable, as bizarre and unfortunate.

At worst, they demonstrated an at times raw form of institutional sectarianism in the Republic of Ireland of the early 1970s.

Briefly, our business ran into difficulties with a trade union, resulting in a week-long strike, which was resolved temporarily, but it led to a substantial fall-off in business, resulting in the laying off of one worker the following year, in agreement with the union. However, despite the agreement, this lay-off led to further strike action in May 1972. What followed were eight weeks filled with frustration and fear as we tried and failed to resolve the situation.

During all of this time, it became increasingly clear to me and my family that certain elements in the union were acting not out of any great sense of justice, but from a purely sectarian standpoint. This was made clear when one particular member told me that I was a "Protestant bastard" and that they were "going to put me out of business and there was ***** I could do about it". We were also advised that, given the political sensitivities of the time, we would be foolish to seek an injunction against the strike action.

Space does not permit me to tell of the harassment, bomb threats, intimidation, anonymous telephone calls to my family, myself and customers. Suffice to say that despite all the complaints to the Garda over this eight-week period, not one charge was ever laid. With the business ruined, we closed our doors on 2 June 1973.

In 1974 we attempted to take a breach of action against the union. We were told by legal counsel that, in his opinion, the "employment or non-employment of workers is a trade dispute despite any agreements".

I moved to Canada in 1974.

In a recent report on human rights, Ireland has been compared to the Soviet Union of many years ago and has also earned the condemnation of the European Commission against racism and intolerance of its minority religious groups.

I would suggest that the denial of any basic civil human rights to Irish Protestant citizens explains the reluctance of Northern Ireland Protestants to join a united Ireland.

Note: Joe Patterson is at present taking his case to the European Court of Human Rights.

Andy Pollak

Andy Pollak is the director of the Centre for Cross Border Studies in Armagh. Formerly religious affairs and education correspondent of The Irish Times, *he was co-ordinator of the Opsahl Commission in Northern Ireland in the early 1990s. He is co-author of a political biography of Rev Ian Paisley and a former editor of the Belfast magazine* Fortnight. *He is a member of the Dublin Unitarian Church.*

I am not a southern Protestant, but a Northern Protestant with a Jewish father. My home and family are now in Dublin although I still work mostly in the North. Thus, as on most issues to do with religion and politics on the island of Ireland, I am an oddball, representing nobody but myself.

However, in the nearly 20 years I have lived in the Republic of Ireland, I have always noticed that one stereotype of southern Protestantism that I had read about appeared to be true. Protestants in the independent Irish State, with a few notable exceptions, keep their heads down when it comes to politics in particular and issues of importance to Irish society in general.

When I first arrived in Dublin in the early 1970s, I was anxious to play my small part as a Protestant citizen of the Republic of Ireland. However, I looked, usually in vain, for Protestants who had made their mark on the new State, whether in politics or public service or journalism or the arts or sport. In those days, businessmen were not idealised as role models the way they have been since the Celtic Tiger, so I did not notice the disproportionately large number of Protestants continuing to prosper quietly in the world of Irish business.

There were few, if any, outspoken or coherent southern Protestant — or, more specifically, Church of Ireland — views on the
burning issues of the day, whether poverty and emigration, taxa-
tion and public spending, abortion and divorce (although this
started to change on these latter issues during the 1983 and 1986
referenda). I was struck how the Dáil in the 1980s contained three
deputies from the tiny Jewish community, but only one, Ivan
Yates, who was a Protestant.

There were, of course, exceptions. Dean Victor Griffin of St
Patrick's Cathedral was a brave and outspoken voice against the
excesses of Catholic-inspired laws on contraception, divorce and
abortion, and the campaigning fundamentalist groups which
wanted those laws maintained or strengthened. David Norris was
a hugely courageous voice for homosexual law reform and other
liberal causes. Douglas Gageby's *Irish Times* was a beacon of liber-
alism and open-mindedness during the early 1980s when a return
to an exclusive, 1950s-style Catholic ethos seemed at times to be a
real possibility.

The reasons why Protestants have played such a very small
part in the public life of the Republic of Ireland have often been
stated. Some argue that it is because they have always been a
small minority cowed by a large majority determined to enforce a
conservative Catholic ethos on the new State. Others say that they
have always been comfortably off and have never had any reason
to rock the boat. A third view is that they have never really identified with the State and for that reason have not become seriously
involved in politics or public life.

Over the past 30 years, matters have improved somewhat. A
few more southern Protestant heads have appeared prominently
above the parapet: people like the civil servant and senator Martin
Mansergh, the judges Susan Denham and Catherine McGuinness,
the Green politician Trevor Sargent, the trade unionist Chris Hud-
son, the farmers' leader Alan Gillis and GAA president Jack
Boothman.

In the past decade, there has been an even more marked
change, as organised religion in general has become less impor-

tant in people's lives; the Republic has become one of Europe's most economically successful States; and a younger generation of southern Protestants has found it easy to identify with the more optimistic, pluralist and cosmopolitan atmosphere of Ireland at the turn of the twenty-first century.

Call me an impossible idealist, but now I believe it is time for Protestant attitudes to move on again. It is one thing to identify with the country you were born and reared in because you are making successful living out of it. It is quite another to express your solidarity with your fellow-citizens by putting something back into it through public or community service, or at least contributing your critical voice to the public debate about the shape it is taking and the directions it is going.

The former Church of Ireland Archbishop of Dublin, Dr Walton Empey, said something similar in his farewell address. He said southern Protestants were loyal citizens of the Irish State, and as such it was incumbent on them to let their views be known — "if we do not, we can hardly complain that our voice is never heard". He went on: "We love our country, we are proud to be Irish. When we speak out, let it be in that knowledge, for that will change our tone from one of minority whinging to loving criticism, which is a very different matter altogether."

Northern Protestants need to hear that southern Protestant voice too. They particularly need to hear it in the public debate which must begin one of these days about what it means to be Irish in the first decades of the new century. The old twentieth-century definition of Irishness — exclusive, narrowly Catholic, paying lip-service to the Irish language, anti-English, often tolerant of murder and mayhem in its name — has served this island badly in the last three decades.

The highly educated young people who will one day soon take over the running of this newly wealthy State subscribe to few of these stale and xenophobic old shibboleths. They are utterly uninterested in tribal brawls on the streets of Belfast. Their dilemmas will be different. They will be faced with the huge task of formulating a new definition of Irishness in an expanded European

Union and a globalised world, one that can incorporate racial and religious minorities from a wide range of different cultures — not just Northern Protestants — into a socially just, multicultural society.

I hope a new generation of young Irish Protestants, unencumbered by the fears and timidities of their parents and grandparents, will draw from their experience of minority status to contribute forcefully to this debate. I hope they will gain inspiration from the writings of courageous Irish Protestant internationalists like George Bernard Shaw and Hubert Butler and realise that love of one's own country can be a joyful step towards embracing and understanding the wider world, rather than — as it has been too often in this country — a retreat into arid insularity.

I hope they will learn to echo that great Lutheran statesman from Sweden, former UN Secretary General Dag Hammarskjöld, whose family tree of soldiers and ministers of religion was so similar to that of many Irish Protestants. From his father, he learned that "no life was more satisfactory than one of selfless service to your country — or to humanity". From his mother he learned that "in the very radical sense of the Gospels, all men were created equal as children of God". Now there's a patriotism and a Protestantism one could be proud of.

Homan Potterton

*Homan Potterton was born in 1946. A gradu-
ate of Trinity College, Dublin and of the University of Edinburgh, he was Director of the
National Gallery of Ireland from 1980–88. He
currently lives in rural France. In 2001, his
memoirs,* Rathcormick, *were published by
New Island Books. The book describes a 1950s
childhood in a "Big House" surrounded by a
300-year-old farm which his parents inherited.
The following is an extract from* Rathcormick
and is reproduced with the kind permission of New Island Books.

"One of Our Own"

Mr Hannigan was one of a series of secretaries — each one
more disastrous than the preceding — employed by Papa in
the interim between the departure of Miss Shannon (a gem) and
the arrival of Mr Denning (another gem). These secretaries always
lived with us, occupying the small bedroom between the nursery
(by then also a bedroom) and the boys' room on the top floor.
They took all their meals with us, were required to play tennis,
croquet, whist or Monopoly (above all, Monopoly) with us and, in
general, were counted upon to become part of the family. These
prerequisites, however, did not allow them scope for any familiarity: Papa's secretaries were always called solely by their surnames
— prefaced by Miss or Mr — and they in turn, like the men in the
yard or the maids in the kitchen, were expected to refer to Papa
and Mamma only as the Master and the Mistress. Once they were
installed at Rathcormick, they had little opportunity for escape —
it would have been unheard of then for someone in such a
position to have their own car — so it was essential that they

would find the notion of an isolated life in the country among a family of boys and an invalid sister reasonably attractive. They were not permitted to smoke and, if they met all the other requirements, it was unlikely that they would have ever even heard of alcohol.

With such unusual criteria, it followed that it was not always easy for Papa to find secretaries and by the same token those who accepted such extraordinary conditions were, almost by definition, in some way extraordinary themselves. The advertisement for the post in *The Irish Times*, calling for a "lady . . . office-general, live-in", would specify that it was a "country position". It would also declare: "C of I preferred". This reference to religion — to the Protestant Church of Ireland — was not intended as a ban on Catholic candidates but as a signal which, when read in conjunction with the words "live-in", would make plain what it was that lay in store for the successful applicant.

At this time in Ireland, most Protestants and Catholics observed their religion. They went to church every Sunday and most practised their respective faiths in the home as well. While we would say grace before and after meals, we did not bless ourselves as Catholics did; and while we often had communal prayers at home, we did not observe the angelus by stopping for silent prayer twice a day on hearing a chapel bell. Catholics, we thought, took the name of the Lord in vain. "Holy God!" they would say with equanimity, and nor did they keep holy the Sabbath day. Protestants observed it as a day of rest which meant that even playing tennis — much less cards or organised team sports — was out of the question, whereas Catholics reserved Sundays almost exclusively for sport. They played Gaelic football and hurling (which Protestants never did) and on Sunday nights, in what seemed like a terrible sin to us, they went to dances.

On a secular level, thrift, or Protestant meanness, was endemic to our way of life — from using up leftovers in the kitchen to "turning" bed sheets and worn collars on shirts — while waste and extravagance, synonymous in our view with a Catholic way of life, were deplored by us. There are countless other examples of how Catholics and Protestants behaved and thought differently and, as a result, a degree of segregation, accepted by most without any fundamental sectarian antagonism, became an inevitable social convention. We referred to another Protestant as "one of our own" and Catholics, no doubt, had a similar euphemism for one of theirs. Protestants, as the expression went, "dug with one foot"; Catholics, very decidedly, with the other. In the context of these customs, these restrictions, it is extremely unlikely that any Catholic would have been comfortable living among us at Rathcormick and it was for that reason — as much as our own possible discomfort in being confronted by Catholicism at such close quarters — that Papa sought, and always found, a Protestant secretary.

Hilary Pratt

Hilary Pratt has been Executive Director of Avoca Handweavers since 1974, after spending 13 years as a secondary school teacher in Dublin. She was educated at Hall School in Monkstown, St Leonard's School, St Andrews in Scotland and at Trinity College, Dublin. She is married to Donald Pratt and has five children and three grandchildren.

My mother's family was of English and Scottish stock, farming in Wicklow and Kildare for 300 years. My father's family was Irish, one of the Galway Tribes, turned Protestant in the seventeenth century — no doubt for reasons of expediency and the Penal Laws. My parents had grown up in Dublin during the turbulent years, 1916–22. My father's family were deeply divided in their Civil War loyalties. As a child, I remember fierce arguments as his siblings, who were working abroad, came home on holidays to relive the conflict!

My parents took the decision not to have their children baptised, believing that religion had been such a divisive element in Ireland. Neither were they church-goers — the first time I saw them in church was at my sister's wedding! It didn't matter. We were known to be Protestants, labelled for life as surely as if we had marks on our foreheads. We were different, and in Ireland in the 1940s and 1950s, there was no getting away from it. Once we moved house and the removal van had barely left when a note came through the letter box looking for a cake for the Church of Ireland fête. How did they know about us? Well, they just did. "You're one of us" was a great expression.

Some friends of ours wrote from abroad to enrol their child in a Protestant boarding school. They wrote "Christian" in the appropriate column on the application form. They got a furious response accusing them of being underhand and dishonest!

There was a Protestant enclave in Dublin — old moneyed families, of which we were not a part — that had controlled the commercial and professional life of the city and now felt beleaguered in an independent Ireland. *Ne Temere* was the big bugbear. It was the reason that Protestant families went to extraordinary lengths to keep their children from mixing with Roman Catholics. There were terrible cases where young people had been disowned by their families for marrying a Catholic. My parents didn't fit into this category. My father's professional and business activities meant that a great many of their friends were Catholic and they wanted their children to be fully integrated into Irish society. Nevertheless, as children all our friends were Protestant, probably because we went to Protestant schools, first in Dublin and then in Scotland and afterwards to Trinity College where, because of "the Ban" imposed by Archbishop McQuaid, most of our fellow students were Protestant. Not, I imagine, that Catholics were any keener to mix and marry with us, destined as we were for hellfire or in the case of us poor, unbaptised creatures, for that unsatisfactory place called "Limbo"! Catholic boys did sometimes ask us out, hoping, no doubt, that we might be "chancy". I suspect we were a grave disappointment!

My upbringing differed from that of Catholic children, not least because of a total absence of any religious influence in my home. As a teenager, I was aware of the stranglehold exercised by the Catholic Church over its flock and I remember the feeling of exhilaration, knowing that it had no jurisdiction over me. The fact that Catholic teaching spilt over into the laws of the land so that contraception and divorce were illegal might have annoyed Protestants but the proximity of England made them no more than minor irritants. Later in my life, when I became an active feminist, I fought against such laws, but by then I was fighting alongside my Roman Catholic sisters.

The year 1970 was a watershed in my life. Like most Southerners I was strangely detached from events in Northern Ireland and
until the Civil Rights movement highlighted the situation, I had
no idea of the level of discrimination against Roman Catholics.
For someone brought up to believe in British justice, it was difficult to come to terms with duplicity, propaganda and downright
injustice just a stone's throw from Westminster. I felt no empathy
with the Northern Protestants — those sad beleaguered people —
and they certainly didn't like me. At a conference in Boston in
1973, a unionist woman shouted at me, "Woman, you've been
decimated — have you no sense of outrage?" To them, the southern Protestants had thrown in the towel!

In the 1970s and 1980s I was deeply involved in the women's
movement and at the same time with the fight for multi-
denominational education. My children were at the Church of Ireland national school where an enlightened principal and rector
welcomed children of all religions. The crackdown by the church
authorities led a group to look for a system of national schools not
controlled by the churches. After years of political footballing and
fundraising, the first multi-denominational national school was
opened, since followed by 18 others — all highly successful and
with long waiting lists.

I don't think I ever felt discriminated against because I was
Protestant; different, certainly, but no more. I may be naïve, but I
believe that had I opted for a career in politics, being a Protestant
would not have mattered. My father developed a very successful
solicitor's practice in the 1930s and 1940s. He often told me that
Catholics came to him because they thought as a Protestant he
would be honest. My husband and brothers, also solicitors, had
the same experience. In my own family business, we have never
been aware of any resentment on religious grounds.

In my lifetime, Ireland has changed enormously. It was a painful transition that had to be gone through to exorcise the demons
of conquest, humiliation and famine. Our young people are surg-
ing forward. They have no interest in old hatreds (they may find
new ones of their own). Three of my children have married

Roman Catholics and apart from really liking their choice of partners, I am pleased because it shows they were raised in an atmosphere of tolerance. I used to hate it when as a Protestant I was considered less than Irish. It seemed so narrow and so unfair and served to deny the contribution of all those Protestant Irishmen and women who had fought for Ireland's freedom. I also hated it when Irish people wouldn't wear the poppy on Remembrance Day. Sixty thousand Irishmen died in that horrific conflict and to refuse to honour their memory because they fought under an English flag seems so churlish. Now that I am older, I understand that time alone can heal wounds and ease old hatreds. To most Irish people, Protestantism was synonymous with the oppressor — and now that I accept it, it doesn't matter any more!

Walter Pringle

Walter Pringle has lived and worked in County Monaghan all of his life. He is married to Margaret and they have two sons, Keith and Ian. He is an active member of the local community in Clones, having served as chairperson of several committees, including Clones Community Forum Ltd. and Clones Special Olympics Committee. Walter and his wife are both lay ministers with the Church of Ireland. He also manages to find time to farm part-time and is currently studying for a Certificate in Management Practice with the University of Ulster.

Born on a farm near Clones in an area with almost no neighbours from the minority community, I went to the local Catholic primary school, as the older members of my family had done for their earlier years of primary education. I started school before I was four years old, owing to the sudden death of my father and the fact that my Mum had to take on his role on the farm. Soon I realised that only my brother and myself and another girl who didn't attend regularly belonged to the "Protestants". The Catholic priest, an old Canon, used to come to lead the prayers and his first command was "put out the Protestants" (we had to leave during prayers even when the Canon wasn't in).

My memories are that the other children, who became my friends, felt sympathy for me that I didn't belong to their faith. Probably while I was still very young, I too felt sorrow that I wasn't in this "right" faith but I could do nothing about it. I had to accept that I was alone and unfortunate not to be a Catholic and as a result I was inferior. That is something that even to this day I've never been totally able to shake off.

I learned to ride a bicycle and moved to the nearest Church of Ireland school when I was about 10 or 11 years old. It was almost three miles away, a long distance in the rain and cold. I did not know any of the other children nor where they lived nor their parents. They had all been at the school from the start. Now I had "blown in" to experience more isolation to a school that had one teacher, in an old building, on the second floor up old stone steps. Why wasn't I a Catholic? I had at least felt part of the school I had started in, which had two teachers and a reasonable building. Oh! the poverty in the 1950s, my Dad having died in 1951. I often had to wear clothes passed on from my only two cousins, both girls, which didn't help my inferiority complex.

Clones High School was my next step, an urban school separated from a large housing estate by a high wall. This was the only secondary school in the locality at the time and it was with great difficulty that my Mum saved for the fees. I found myself accepting, as I had experienced in the other schools, that I was at the bottom of the pile. On the occasions we had to cross the wall into the housing estate, where the community was totally from the Catholic tradition, we did so with fear.

As teenagers, we didn't have any opportunity to socialise. The only venue for the community was a little tin hall and I can remember being allowed to attend a bazaar there on one occasion and feeling everyone there was looking at me, the only Protestant attending, raising money for the Catholic Church. This type of function was totally contrary to the minority ethos and although I pleaded with my Mum to let me go I didn't want to go back.

When I first took on off-farm employment it was to work with CIE, as it was then known. My first posting with them was in County Cavan. Nobody knew me. There were seven other drivers. Questions were asked: What was my name? Where did I live? Soon I felt, *they'll know what I am* — not one of them.

My wife works in the Sacred Heart Nursing Home from time to time. She hears the elderly residents saying to each other "she's a Protestant". Did that have anything to do with the job she was employed to do?

I was an elected member of Monaghan County Council (non-party) from 1991 to 1999. Being non-party is probably a lonely road for anyone in politics but to be a non-party Protestant in a County Council along the border where many years ago non-party Protestant public representatives were members of the Protestant Association was even more lonely. Comments from my fellow councillors like "If you don't feel comfortable you should get out" are difficult to forget.

My work with Clones Urban District Council brings me into many homes. Recently, I was in the home of a widowed lady. Her son was talking to someone else in the house about employment. Referring to a certain company, he said, "I wouldn't work there, it's full of f****** Orangemen." At which his Mum looked at me and said, "That's some chat to be at." Why did he make such a remark? How do you think it made me feel?

I'm involved with a community group and I know at that level and at national level our government are seeking to care for minorities. Who are these minorities? Travellers? Romanians? Are we, the Protestant community, not a minority? Should we not be recognised by our government in the same way as the other minorities?

Heather Robinson

Heather Robinson was born and grew up on the northside of Dublin. She attended the High School in Rathgar and studied in UCD, where she gained a Master's Degree in Equality Studies. She has worked with locally based community groups in Glasgow, Dublin and Wiltshire in England. She is presently training as a solicitor in Dublin.

Listening to *Playback* of a Saturday morning on RTE Radio, I am still intrigued at the diversity of "Irishness" highlighted in the various programmes through the week. At the same time, I find myself listening keenly for interesting comments about Protestants and the different perceptions of them sometimes given inadvertently. As such, these differences of experience and culture within Irish society remain, although there are fewer implications from such differences now than in previous decades. This Ireland then, wavering between a non-sectarian political correctness and a platform for all opinions, is also a culture that remains alien to me and within which my family and community have played little part over the past years.

The fact that I only tune in to RTE (unlike the BBC) maybe once a week is illustrative of the point that I feel the need to know more of this country I live in and also that I often find its narrow focus excluding and unsympathetic. It is the experience of such aspects of Irish culture more as a tourist than as a participant that can even today lead to alienation for someone born and brought up in Dublin. This stems even from my primary school where we spent the odd hour or two learning a few steps of Irish dancing more for the experience of it than for the fact that it was a part of Irish heritage.

Learning about being Irish rather than living as someone automatically included within that defined society was again normal for my classmates and myself. My life was filled with completely different activities, many of which were attached to the church that I attended.

An example of such activity that it is hard to describe to anyone who has not been a part of it was my membership of the Girls' Brigade (GB) which I attended for 14 years from the age of two. This is an organisation run entirely by women, which traces its roots back to the Edwardian era, when it was thought progressive that women should be involved in light exercise, in learning scripture and personal discipline, all with a military overtone. It still flourishes today and during my years of membership these aims had remained little changed.

Describing the GB to non-participants is almost impossible and I well remember the one time we had a combined Youth Day activity with the Girl Scouts. The scouts laughed loud and long at our pinafores and white plimsolls and I realised then that the GB may strike outsiders as somewhat different. Yet the GB was in its place a supportive organisation for many women as they were able to assert themselves with the Protestant community after the dramatic loss of men through the First World War. It remains today an organisation where mothers are able to take their daughters and meet each other on a Saturday afternoon.

However, I would not like to build an initial picture that I am indeed a "West Brit" who, caught between two cultures, finds her comfort in neither. I am more than happy to be Irish but cannot define it narrowly as a set of experiences that one ticks off throughout life. Such issues of identity have always held a fascination for me.

Thus being part of the Protestant community and the diversity within that small group in the south of Ireland is where instead my identity is found and reinforced. Within it there is an ease and an immediate understanding, an unspoken shared experience which needs no explanation. This is in contrast to the company of non-Protestant friends, where I feel the need to be more cautious, to explain experiences and above all to cultivate a carefulness, not so much to avoid causing offence as to try and play down your "otherness" or to leave yourself open to the criticism that you are talking of a certain issue because of your background. In some cases, any explanation is fruitless when talking of activities that were the norm in your childhood, so different is my experience from theirs, whereas these are automatically recognised by a Protestant friend.

However, given the size of the Protestant community in the south, it is obvious that in order to socialise it is necessary for its members to travel to be together. Thus the concept of a local parish is something very different to me from the norm. My church, of Presbyterian denomination and based in the city centre, necessitated its members travelling to it from as far as Swords and Wicklow, so that the parish effectively stretched across the city. All activities in my life at that time, from school to youth club, would involve commuting and I was never involved in anything locally based.

Being part of the Presbyterian community within Protestantism is another separate identity, although Church of Ireland and Methodist members would also experience the same issues in terms of separate schools and travel. But Presbyterians were never part of the Anglo-Irish ascendancy or the ruling class of the era under the British. They formed mainly the middle and lower middle classes involved in trade and the professions and such divisions, although rare, are still felt a little today in the contrast of experience between the members of the Church of Ireland and the Dissenters.

These experiences growing up in a community that has a different way of expressing its Irishness have been valuable to me and to be a part of the same community could also be of benefit to the next generation of young Protestants. I enjoy the enrichment this diversity brings to Irish society and the fact that organisations such as the GB have survived the last century in the south is a hopeful sign that Ireland will further embrace the new cultures that are starting to have an impact on life here.

Máire Roycroft

Máire Roycroft BA H.Dip.Ed. M.Ed., a native of west Cork, is a principal teacher of an 11-teacher school in Cork. She began her teaching career in St Luke's School, Douglas, in 1969, and was appointed principal two years later. She served on the INTO Education Committee, the Church of Ireland Diocesan Board of Education, the Irish Committee of the National Council for Curriculum and Assessment and as secretary and chairperson of the Irish Primary Principals Network in Cork.

I spent the first eight years of my life in Leap, County Cork, the third of six children reared on a small farm. Despite the fact that there was a good community spirit in the area, I must confess that I can clearly recollect causing some disharmony with a local family when we called one another names on the way home from school. It is amazing that children have such a deep sense of the religious divide between Roman Catholic and Protestant. Some of my early recollections include accompanying my mother to neighbours' houses helping with the preparations for the traditional station Mass when the priest celebrated Mass in the houses. The celebrations continued all night with dancing, drinking and eating. Another great social occasion was the harvest when a *meitheal* of local farmers of all denominations came to help with the threshing of the corn; the night was spent celebrating — dancing the half-set and finishing the keg of porter. The highlight for the children was the bottle of white lemonade — a real treat.

Because of proximity, I attended the local Roman Catholic primary school. I remember my sense of achievement when I got a prize for Irish in first class, a fact that influenced my love of Irish for the rest of my life. Times were hard for all small farmers in west Cork; nobody had electricity or running water in the 1950s. It was hard to eke out an existence; money was scarce. My mother, like all the farmers' wives, augmented the family income by selling eggs every week; turkeys were reared to be sold at Christmas to pay for the expenses of the festive season; vegetables were grown to feed the family. All the children had chores to do on the farm before they went to school and again in the evenings; homework may not have been accorded the importance we give it today.

Many families, including ours, depended on the parcels of clothes that came annually from neighbours who had emigrated to America and did not forget the poverty at home. These clothes were then taken to the dressmaker to be remodelled to fit the various members of the household. My parents never owned a car; our mode of transport to church every Sunday was by horse and trap until one of my older brothers got a car when he became a motor mechanic.

My younger brother and I spent some months in Buckingham House School (an orphanage which provided a home for children when they could not be cared for at home for whatever reason) when my mother was undergoing surgery in Dublin for a brain tumour. The family was divided for a time, as the six children ranged in ages from one month to 12 years of age. When I was eight years old, the family moved to Ballydehob where we attended the local Church of Ireland two-teacher parish school. As free secondary education had not yet been introduced, the principal prepared some of the senior pupils for various scholarship examinations to schools such as The Collegiate School in Celbridge, King's Hospital, Bandon Grammar School and the preparatory college, Coláiste Moibhí. The majority of pupils left school at the age of 13 or 14 and went to work on the family farm, or local garage, or learned a trade. Protestant boarding schools such as Bandon Grammar School, Midleton College and Rochelle School were in existence but the majority of the Church of Ireland farming community could not afford the fees — even if scholarships were offered. I was lucky that I was accepted into Coláiste Moibhí in 1963 to begin my four-year secondary education, which prepared us for the Leaving Certificate and subsequent entry to the two-year training in the Church of Ireland College of Education.

Our primary school principal, Mr Pollard, a Kerryman, had a great love of Irish and engendered that love in his students. Preparatory colleges were established in 1926 to ensure that primary teachers had the necessary standard of Irish to teach the subject adequately. Although a fee was charged, the school was highly subsidised by the State. The majority of the students came from similar rural backgrounds, mainly Donegal, Cork, Kerry, Cavan and Monaghan. It was a good system at the time as many young Church of Ireland people would not otherwise have received a secondary education. We soon developed a fluency in Irish and the commitment of the staff of the school fostered an interest in Irish culture, dancing, drama and literature. We attended the Irish services once a month in Christ Church Cathedral.

During our period of training in the Church of Ireland Training College, students were obliged to spend a month in the Gaeltacht improving their standard of Irish. Four of our class opted to spend the month of June 1968 on Oileán Cléire off the West Cork Coast where we met members of the *campaí oibre* — voluntary workers, initially mainly clerical students from St Patrick's College Maynooth who spent some weeks of their summers helping the community in various ways, e.g. laying a water scheme and building a museum. The aims of the *campaí oibre* were to speak Irish in the Gaeltacht and to work on voluntary schemes helping both the economic development of the area and the strengthening of the Irish language. As the *campaí oibre* developed over the years, they attracted young people from all denominations and all walks of life. We established a café and organised Irish language courses for students which raised approximately £50,000 over the years to help the local co-op to run an electricity scheme on the island. Irish was the only medium of communication; we made lifelong friends there who shared a common interest in the love of the Irish language. It enriched me as a teacher and my career and the education of the pupils I taught was certainly enhanced. This experience broadened my outlook in life, focusing my attention on the wider community, not just the narrow Church of Ireland dimension to which I might otherwise have confined myself. I was greatly honoured when my work for the Irish language and the Gaeltacht was recognised by my fellow voluntary workers when they nominated me for a Rehab Ireland "Person of the Year Award" in 1978.

I classify myself as a typical ordinary member of the Church of Ireland of rural west Cork — no different from the other members of the Roman Catholic community among whom I grew up. It was a struggle surviving in the country — no luxuries, not even the basic necessities at times. As I grew up, there was an understanding that we attended the Church of Ireland socials — indeed they were the highlight of our Friday nights around the diocese — as it was hoped we would meet a partner of our own faith. During the 1960s and 1970s, the *Ne Temere* decree imposed by the Roman Catholic Church decimated the Church of Ireland population as the children of "mixed" marriages had to be reared in the Roman Catholic faith. We isolated ourselves into ghettoes in the hope of maintaining the Church of Ireland community. It is hard trying to survive as a community when we are such a tiny minority. We did not often play a full role in the community for fear it would lead to more inter-church marriages. People of different faiths should endeavour to live in the community, show mutual respect for one another, respect their rights to religious liberty, participate fully in the local community and respect one another's differences. This is surely better than the isolation the Church of Ireland minority imposed on itself, which was nevertheless understandable. Even though the Roman Catholic partner in an inter-Church marriage still has to promise to do their utmost to bring up the children in the Roman Catholic faith, many couples decide for themselves nowadays what faith they wish to pass on to their children.

I have never experienced discrimination. In reality, I was always given a special welcome just because I was a member of the minority but we are still seen as "different", not quite Irish. Members of the Church of Ireland have a responsibility to participate fully in the community to ensure that we have an open, egalitarian society. There are those out there who still think we are all West Brits, born with a silver spoon in our mouths, speak with cultured accents, and come from privileged backgrounds. I speak on behalf of the many, many ordinary Irish Church of Ireland folk whose only difference from their neighbours is that they go to a different church on Sunday. We are proud of our country and of our rich cultural heritage.

To quote Thomas Davis, the editor of *The Nation* and a member of the Church of Ireland, "Breathes there a man with soul so dead who never to himself has said, 'This is my own, my native land.'"

Fergus Ryan

Captain Fergus Ryan retired from Aer Lingus in 1993. He is the leader of Trinity Church Network in Dublin, one of the largest of the Republic's "New Churches". He is married to Sarah, and has four daughters. Fergus is also an artist.

Altered State

Nobody from either family came to the wedding at St George's in Temple Street. The year 1938 was only 17 short years after the War of Independence and my parents' mixed marriage in one of the largest Church of Ireland parishes in the Free State was still a bridge uncrossable from either end. Clare's father had joined the army in the Great War while at home the Empire's second city convulsed in revolution. Laurence's father's house in Goldsmith Street had been raided by Black and Tans looking for republican guns. His sister Anna, a senior medical officer in *Cumann na mBan*, had accompanied de Valera and the Archbishop when they visited the families of the Volunteers executed by the British in the War of Independence. His brother had been arrested by soldiers on his way to Boland's Mill with a message for de Valera's forces, but had escaped execution because the tightly rolled paper had fallen through a hole in his trouser pocket. In the Civil War that followed the establishment of the new State, it was Anna who brought de Valera's wreath to Michael Collins's funeral in a dangerous car dash in County Cork.

The memories lay crouching under the fluted Ionic columns of Francis Johnston's St George's, ensuring that no one entered.

*   *   *

The Corporation estate in Cabra where we grew up was a long way from the grandeur of Croydon House in Philipsburg Avenue where my mother had lived, but I wasn't aware of that. We were as hard-pressed as everyone else in the late 1940s and 1950s. What I was sharply aware of was that we were "different". On the road, there were real friendships, but there were also the regular taunts of "proddy-woddy" from some of the bullies, not all of whom were children. My playmate Peter was breaking the rules because the priest had told him that "one bad apple makes the whole barrel bad", and I was a bad apple. The Legion of Mary regularly called to warn my father of the "illegitimacy" of his four children (it was put more forcefully) since his marriage in the Church of Ireland was "invalid". It was a matter of some bemusement to the women on the No. 12 bus that there were only three children in my class at Blaquiere Bridge school, but I informed them that we got "great individual attention"! When one elderly neighbour died, we were ushered up to the candled and shaded bedroom to see the corpse. Suddenly from behind the door a voice that seemed to come from the grave boomed, "Get down there on your knees and say three Our Fathers and three Hail Marys!" It was (although I didn't know it) the local priest. We collapsed in fright and, shuddering, muttered the Lord's Prayer, complete with the giveaway longer ending. On the way down the stairs, I said loudly to my older sisters, "Who's your man and what's a Hail Mary?"

Life for us centred on the parish and its mosaic of organisations. In Sunday school and in Boys' Brigade, we were taught obedience and discipline, how to read the Bible, practical skills of all kinds and, especially, brass band music. I was appointed to the exalted office of company bugler to play the "Last Post" at the annual Remembrance Day service in the parish, and to the even more elevated position of assistant steeple-keeper, travelling with the older campanologists to places as far away as Doneraile in County Cork to ring the peals of bells.

But my father was not part of this world and he never came to church events. Through influences from the Writers' Club in London, he had become a member of the Irish branch of the Theosophical Society, a spiritualist movement started in the previous century by Madam Helena Blavatsky and associated in Ireland with W.B. Yeats and the Golden Dawn. His very private bedroom was a mysterious, musty place filled with old books, none of which was Christian — *Esoteric Buddhism, The Light of Asia, The Kabala, The Koran*; books of pantheistic poetry, gnostic secrets, arcane symbols, faeries, and ancient Sanskrit; Goëthe, Uhlands and Schiller in old German text; and works on Freudian "analysis". He introduced me to the world of the poets Jonathan Hanaghan and Rupert Strong at Mount Town House, near Monkstown. When I was about 12, he brought me to the India Tea Centre in Suffolk Street to see a film about the ritual bathings in the Ganges and to meet his Indian friends. He talked about reincarnation and levitation, and projected thoughts to us from another room. Before he died when I was 14 he had become, in effect, a Hindu. My mother didn't think that anyone called Ryan could be a Hindu. At the chapel at Mount Jerome Cemetery that cold day in 1962, a small group entered to hear the few words spoken. Most of his relatives stayed outside.

*   *   *

"Are you a Christian?" the girl on O'Connell Street asked me. She was a friend of my sister, from Glasnevin parish, and she was with a group of people who seemed to be preaching on the street. It was the summer of 1965.

"What do you think I am — a Buddhist?" I said, missing the irony. She told me she had become a Christian. I asked her what Church she belonged to now. "Church of Ireland, still. Do you know Jesus?"

"What? Sure he's dead!"

She invited me to go to a prayer meeting in Rathgar the following day. It was in the home of a Baptist minister, a species of Protestant with which I was unfamiliar, but I found the event strangely agreeable. That evening we went to a meeting in Merrion Hall, a Brethren Assembly. I knew nothing then of the Church of Ireland origins of the movement in Powerscourt in the 1820s. Jesus and the cross seemed to receive more attention than I was used to, and things I had heard all my life took on a new light. At midnight, a divine transaction took place beside my bed in Cabra.

"I've become a committed Christian," I told my headmaster a few days later after RE class. He lit his pipe slowly without responding. Then, as if through the smoke from some altar of incense, "I can see the Evangelicals have been getting at you." I didn't know anything about Evangelicals, Anglican or otherwise. "I bet you twenty quid, Fergy, in ten years you'll have forgotten the whole thing."

*   *   *

It was a warm Sunday in October 2001. I stepped out of the Evangelical church in Lower Abbey Street. Things had changed; not many of the now several hundred members were from a Protestant background. From the direction of O'Connell Bridge, a rippling and pounding slow-march drum beat reverberated and bounced through the city's streets and I shivered unexpectedly in the Indian summer. In light that seemed to come from the sun of another time, ten hearses with the exhumed remains of the Volunteers executed by the British in the War of Independence crept past the great fluted Ionic columns of Francis Johnston's General Post Office in a surreal military drama suffused with subversive memories. I felt strangely confused, alienated, fearful, as if suddenly caught in a warp of years, an altered state. Just up the road, near the Garden of Remembrance, the deconsecrated St George's was preparing its plush bars and dancefloor for the Sunday evening faithful.

John Bartley Shannon

*John Bartley Shannon was born at Dar-
raghlan, Stranoodan, County Monaghan
on 14 May 1912. He attended Urcher National School from 1916 to 1926, then
Monaghan Model School until 1930 when
he entered Kildare Place, Church of Ireland Training College by Easter Scholarship Examination. On account of the
College's connection with Trinity College
Dublin, he later obtained the Degrees of
BA and MA. In 1933, he was appointed teacher of St Johnston No. 1
National School, County Donegal, and taught there until 1975 when the
school was amalgamated with Monreagh NS. He retired in 1977, having
completed 45 years in service.*

Having been at national school in 1923, I was in the first class
to embark on the study of the Irish language, which I have
been learning, teaching and speaking ever since.

My ancestors being Presbyterian for many generations, I was
brought up as part of the Presbyterian Church, Cahans, in County
Monaghan.

As a teacher in the school under the management of St Johnston Presbyterian Church, I have been involved in Church activities, including assisting in helping returned members from
Australia and America in working out connections with their ancestors and also interpreting local history, in which I have made
full use of the erudition of Rev A.G. Lecky of Ballylennon, who
wrote two books in 1905 and 1908 about "Roots of Presbyterianism in County Donegal". For my services to local history, geneal-
ogy and folklore, I was awarded a Doctorate in Literature by
Dublin Metropolitan University.

The recollections of events are very clear in my mind. For instance, I remember very well the talk the teacher gave about the formation of the Garda Síochána in 1924; how she portrayed the marvellous courage of all those men who volunteered to join an unarmed force — there were to be 5,000 instead of the force of about 7,000 in the RIC and Auxiliaries. They succeeded very well and became a very good police force.

Many Protestants have served in this force down through the years. They became very well known to all the people when they collected agricultural statistics and distributed Census forms, etc. It seems to me to have been a mistake to alter their pattern of work, which was done by foot patrols and bicycles.

In the early days of the State, we rejoiced in the recognition of W.B. Yeats, the Protestant poet who won the Nobel Prize for Literature in 1923; and by learning Irish poetry, we became acquainted with Douglas Hyde in the Glen in which he was born: *An Gleann nar togadh mé*. He was to become the first President in 1938 after the adoption of the Constitution in 1937.

Having celebrated my ninetieth birthday this year, I can remember all the following events: the Truce of 11 July 1921 and the signing of the Treaty on 6 December 1921, which brought to an end a period of turbulence and strife which had existed in various degrees of intensity from 1916 when the Easter Rebellion occurred. On 7 January 1922, the Irish Free State came into being on the Ratification of the Treaty by 64 votes to 57, a very slender majority. Those who concurred with and agreed to its terms were very glad that peace had been restored. Those who disagreed immediately left the Dáil, led by Eamon de Valera.

W.T. Cosgrove formed a Cumann na nGaedhael Government in 1923 but the Civil War ensued and many coercion laws were put in place to restore law and order. This Government remained in power from 1923 until 1932. The Protestants were greatly disappointed, especially those living in Donegal, Monaghan and Cavan, with having been excluded from the regime envisaged in the Solemn League and Covenant of 28 September 1912, but became exemplary citizens, upholding the law and progressing in their lawful pursuits and businesses.

Who were those Protestants and from whence had they come? They came to Ireland from England, Scotland and France. From England they came to Cork in the reign of Elizabeth I (1558–1603). Then there were the Plantations of Laois and Offaly and, most notably, the Plantation of Ulster in the reign of James I (1603–1625). The Scottish Presbyterians landed at Carrickfergus in 1642 in the army of General Munroe, who came to quell the Rebellion of 1641. They founded the First Presbyterian Congregation in Ireland in Carrickfergus and then came westwards to Derry and Donegal, founding Monreagh in 1644. Great multitudes of French Huguenots came in several waves of immigration after the massacre of St Bartholomew's Day in 1572, the fall of La Rochelle in 1628, but the largest contingent came after the Revocation of the Edict of Nantes in 1685; many of this latter group were deeply involved in the Williamite Wars (1688–1691).

The Plantation of Ulster which followed the Flight of the Earls in 1607 was the most successful of the many which took place and Scottish immigrants made great progress in agriculture, notably flax-growing and the establishment of the linen industry; the Huguenots from France settled mostly in Dublin, the West of Ireland and Portadown in County Armagh where they developed such industries as silk and poplin, and many developed commercial and banking interests.

With the establishment of the Irish Free State in 1922, a major change took place in education. The policy of the new regime was the restoration of the Irish language. They declared that they thought this would be possible in 25 years. Many problems confronted the schools because very few of the teachers knew the language. In the year 1923, a crash course was put in place all over the country and everyone who knew Irish was called in as an instructor. The course lasted for six weeks and the holidays for six weeks which meant we had a break of three months from school: a novelty then, a common thing now.

Despite compulsory summer courses for all teachers under 45 years of age, a new source of Irish-speaking teachers was required, considered essential for the success of the language policy. A committee in December 1924 decided that new preparatory colleges should be established, entirely Irish-speaking with the exception of English as a subject.

In 1925, seven colleges were established and the Protestant preparatory college, Coláiste Moibhí, Glasnevin, was established in 1926 and functioned with great success for 40 years, until it was closed down in 1966. By that time, the secondary schools all over the Republic of Ireland were competent to train the recruits for the College of Education, Rathmines, successor to the Church of Ireland Training College, Kildare Street, Dublin.

The new Government in 1922 established border customs "huts", as they were called, for collection of tariffs and prevention of smuggling. They were thought to be of short duration but eventually lasted for 70 years and we were all delighted to see them abolished. Protection for native industries did some good in the border counties; furniture-making flourished in County Monaghan and motor car industries in Dublin and Cork, but cities and towns like Derry, Dundalk, Clones and Monaghan had their hinterland cut off and trade was greatly impeded.

Many families moved to America, Australia, Canada and England to obtain work and the general demographic fluctuation has left much of the countryside today with the distressing vista of abandoned and decaying buildings: Church of Ireland churches, Orange Halls, derelict national schools, obsolete flax and oat mills. No adverse laws were ever passed which caused all these things to happen but the increasing mechanisation of farming left fewer opportunities for agricultural workers and increasing employment in newly founded industrial undertakings has hastened the flight from the land. In the 1920s, there were 800 schools under Church of Ireland management and about 200 under Presbyterian and Methodist patronage. There are much fewer now owing to amalgamation, bussing of pupils, smaller families and movement overseas. The school I attended, Urcher National School, County Monaghan, which had been established in 1812, closed recently.

The Loyal Orange Institution and the Royal Black Preceptories, which had a large membership in Monaghan, Cavan and Donegal, and also in Dublin, Leitrim and Wicklow, held demonstrations regularly in July and August during the years 1922–1931 but they ceased to hold those except in Rossnowlagh and a few times in Raphoe (1943) and St Johnston (1946), all in Co Donegal. Brethren from Cavan, Donegal and Monaghan now travel to the nearest gathering in Northern Ireland. However, recently a number of Orange Brethren celebrated a special occasion by conducting a religious service on the Boyne Battle site. The family atmosphere being enjoyed at these meetings and the lovely music supplied by the various bands are something to be appreciated and admired.

I don't know how we as Protestants have been perceived. It is likely that we would be regarded as not truly Irish but that would be erroneous. We are all anxious to be loyal citizens, acting for and rejoicing in the prosperity and peace of our native land, attending well our churches, listening to our teachings and practising well in the outside world all those virtues which have been inculcated in us.

Canon Hilary Wakeman

Hilary Wakeman is a recently retired priest in the Church of Ireland, and an honorary Canon Emeritus of Norwich Cathedral. She is the founder of the Julian meetings, an ecumenical network of contemplative prayer groups and the editor of Circles of Stillness *(Darton, Longman & Todd, 2002) and* Woman Priests: The First Years *(Darton, Longman & Todd, 2002).*

The Church of Ireland is a lot like my Aunt Nancy. Happening to have been born in England, but then having lived in New York for about 40 years, she was inordinately proud of what she described as "my English accent". To us, it sounded like a strange new construction. It certainly wasn't American, but it wasn't English either.

When I came to Ireland in 1996 as a priest ordained in the Church of England, I imagined that the Church of Ireland would be very Irish in its culture, speech and attitudes. I thought that my Englishness would be an embarrassment and hoped I would naturalise quickly. After all, my mother was from Galway, the Irish blood was there, the voice would surely follow? But it turned out to be more complicated than that.

For a start, my mother is Catholic, and I was raised a Catholic, only leaving the Church in the convinced atheism of my teens. When I came joyfully back into Christianity at the age of 30, it seemed sheer chance that it was into the Anglican Church, the Church of England. In England, the Anglican Church is broad, ranging from very evangelical to very catholic. I tended towards the catholic wing, in my churchgoing and later in my ministry. I was not aware of the problems that this would cause when, fired up by the hope that Christian unity was about to happen in Ireland, I came to work here, where the Anglican Church is not broad at all. "You mustn't wear *that*", my parishioners said when I celebrated the Eucharist in a cassock alb. "You mustn't do *that*", they said when they saw I made the sign of the cross over the congregation. When asked why I mustn't do these and other things, the answer was always, "because *they* do that". The Catholics do that, so we don't. People didn't put it into these words, but it is a matter of retaining tribal identity.

As my first year went by, I began to understand how very different these two Anglican Churches of Ireland and England are. It was educational to move from being a member of the majority Church to being a member of the minority, with all the implications that has for your place in the community; sometimes wooed, sometimes overlooked. But I was depressed by the narrowness, both cultural and theological, of the Church of Ireland; and by what seemed to me to be dull buildings, poor singing, a lack of drama in the liturgy, and a general approach to religion which is more of the head than of the heart. I soon felt starved of all the things in churches that stimulate worship: art, architecture, liturgical movement, music. Above all, I was depressed by the aversion to change. Parishioners were once asked to vote for one of five options regarding the future of a church that was too big and a church hall that was too dilapidated. The chosen course of action was "Do nothing."

The ecumenism that I had come here to be part of turned out to be far more real in the towns and villages than in the churches. From the start, my family and I were wonderfully welcomed by the whole community, and have continued to feel part of it beyond my recent retirement. Yet in the churches, I discovered, congregational exchanges between Catholics and Protestants were token, limited to a few specified occasions every year. I believe the people themselves would be happy with far more interaction but that it is the clergy on both sides who hold back.

How Irish is the Church of Ireland? I still puzzle over this. It is more English that I expected but, like my Aunt Nancy's accent, it bears little relation to current Englishness. In some ways it is better: it already has an informality of relationship between bishops and clergy, and the relationship between men and women in the Church is infinitely better than it is over the water. Churchgoing is still the norm rather than the exception. It is in the expectations of the laity that the Church seems to be in a time warp, no doubt influenced by but also in reaction to Catholic clergy–laity relations. Church of Ireland people see themselves as having in their minister a parent figure, who will spend most of his/her time looking after them, visiting them not just when they are sick or in hospital but on a regular, casual, social basis also. And, like a parent at a school sports day, this parent must make a good impression in the community: must have a big house, nice garden, good clothes, and a car that is neither small nor old.

All of this, even the regularity of church attendance, comes back to the matter of tribal identity. The idea of the wealthy and paternal rector is a throwback to the nineteenth century, and seems to be clung to without the realisation that we are in a different world now. The marked aversion to change and the horror of doing what "they" do comes from fear: the boundaries must be clearly marked if this small Church is not to disappear into Catholicism. This fear is understandable but gives little hope for ecumenism.

My hope for the future lies in a number of factors — economic, pastoral and theological — which suggest that there will be a breakdown soon of inhibiting ecclesiastical structures. Clerical scandals in the Catholic Church and the drastic decrease in the numbers of ordinands led Bishop Willie Walsh to say recently on television that "Local people have to take over ownership of the Church". The Church of Ireland's heresy trial of the Dean of Clonmacnoise was cancelled when he resigned, but he had already shown new ways of expressing old truths which must be found if the Church is to retain its integrity and parishioners. With such vast changes pending it would be surprising if the old sectarian barriers did not simply fall underfoot, unregarded. And what a glory that would be.

Susan Walsh

Susan Walsh, age 30, is a teacher of French and German in Mount Temple Comprehensive School in north Dublin. She lives in Shankill with her husband and two sons.

Being part of the Protestant community in Ireland is a part of my identity, but it doesn't define me in the way it would have previous generations. "The parish" was always part of my life growing up, whether it was Sunday School, Brownies, Guides, youth club discos, the parish fête or whatever, and my experiences as a member of the Church of Ireland have been positive. But I think that I am different to my parents' generation because I feel less threatened by the majority religion, Roman Catholicism, and more integrated and at ease for that reason.

My husband is a Roman Catholic and it is our intention to bring up our children in an interfaith marriage (whatever that term means, and believe me it changes all the time). I am not saying that everything goes swimmingly and that there are not sometimes tensions in relation to religious matters or our different traditions, but overall I would describe myself as proud to be a member of the Church of Ireland whilst comfortable with the religion practised by the majority of people on this island.

Growing up as a Protestant in suburban Dublin in the 1970s and 1980s was really not that different to growing up in any other tradition, as far as I can tell. The parish provided me with an extra set of friends and social life outside of my school and neighbourhood friends, and there was a great sense of community. I still love going back to my original church and being amongst people I have known since I was tiny. I always knew I was part of a minority community in Ireland, but this made me feel special rather than under threat or very different.

Unlike previous generations, I did not mix exclusively with other Protestants. I suppose the proof of this is that, whereas my parents' friends almost all married other Protestants, I have been to nothing but Roman Catholic or interfaith weddings, including my own.

When it came to getting married, things got a little more complicated. We had a lot to work out in order to find a compromise for the wedding, before even starting out on married life. However, the interfaith marriage preparation course was excellent. Sitting beside a Muslim–Jewish couple, we realised that our situation wasn't really complicated at all. The priests, Catholic and Protestant, were really practical and down-to-earth about how to deal with different situations (if you are having difficulty with your local church, shop around) and we have found ourselves using their advice a lot since then, particularly since having our son.

What we are aiming for is to have the best of both worlds — we want our children to feel comfortable and at home in both traditions. We try to go to each church alternately, so that from day one they are used to both.

In many ways, I think we are lucky, as each church has different pros and cons. For example, you get a fantastic welcome at our local Church of Ireland services, purely because of the numbers being smaller. But in the local Roman Catholic church, you get a much more diverse cross-section of society, which is important to us too. This is not always the case in the Church of Ireland; I remember one Sunday years ago in my original parish, I was trying to explain to my husband who was who. "She was the old lady in the tweed suit," I said. "But they were all old ladies in tweed suits," was the reply.

There are aspects of Roman Catholic teaching with which I have difficulty. One issue that has caused us a problem is the communion issue. I would like to receive the Eucharist in the Catholic Church just like anyone else, and don't want our children to wonder why their mother has to be excluded. So we talked to our local priest, who said very openly, "I think this is a case where the boss has got it wrong." Once we realised that the boss he was referring to was the Archbishop (and not God!) we felt that I could receive without feeling that I had anything to hide.

This characterises my experience of the Roman Catholic Church as a Protestant. Some of the priests on the ground are doing fantastic work to make their Church an open, inclusive, vibrant, community-led place, but it appears that this is despite the best efforts of the hierarchy.

The differences in our traditions have always, however, provided us with lots of laughs. Looking through my husband's eyes, I can see the "funny little ways" that I always considered normal — gathering up wrapping paper at Christmas and ironing it ready for next year, never throwing anything out because "you never know when it might come in handy", belting hymns out in full voice regardless of ability to sing, making awful marmalade and chutney, and having your name and parish written on the bottom of trays and tins (for all those sales of work). Our most recent discovery is that in the nursery rhyme "This little piggy went to market", the Protestant third little piggy ate roast beef, whereas the Catholic one ate bread and butter.

So despite the complications, I consider myself lucky to be a member of the Church of Ireland, but doubly lucky to be married to a Roman Catholic — having a foot in both camps may be tricky at times, but I think it enriches our marriage and family life as a result.

Sarah Webb

Sarah Webb, 33, is a writer, a mother and a children's book consultant. She lives in south County Dublin with her son and her partner. She has written three best selling books: Three Times a Lady, Always the Bridesmaid *and* Something to Talk About. *She recently signed a new deal with British publishers, Macmillan, for a further two books. She also writes books for children and attends St Paul's church in Glenageary.*

I had what can only be described as a very happy and somewhat privileged childhood — frightfully unfashionable in this age of Frank McCourt and Nuala O'Faoláin — but true nonetheless. Growing up in Dalkey, south County Dublin, with Church of Ireland parents, grandparents, friends and wider relations, for many years I had no real sense of the larger picture — that being a Protestant in Ireland was actually as rare as hen's teeth. I attended the local Church of Ireland national school, followed by St Andrew's College in Booterstown, then and still a delightfully multicultural and truly multi-denominational school. Here I met boys and girls from many different cultures, many of whom were embassy children and children of international businessmen and women who accompanied their parents all over the world. One of my best friends, Abby, was Jewish and lived in Rathmines; another, Anna, was Swedish and Lutheran; and a third, Carolyn, had been living in Canada for many years and was Roman Catholic. It was during my time at St Andrew's and through my involvement in sailing as a teenager that it began to dawn on me that my "different" Protestant background had shaped my views and most especially my moral outlook. But it was only upon entering college, ironically

Trinity College Dublin, once a "Protestant enclave", that I began to realise that I was indeed hideously outnumbered and that being Protestant in Ireland was something of an oddity.

My grandfather, William Bedell Stanford, was Professor of Greek at Trinity College, Dublin, and later Chancellor. Re-reading his memoirs recently, I was struck by how attitudes towards Protestants have changed since his day. As a child he was taunted in the streets — "Proddy, Proddy, blue guts, never said a prayer, catch him by the left leg, and haul him down the stair." My Roman Catholic friends are by now "honorary" Protestants one and all — many are on first-name terms with my clergyman (and profess not to have even met their own priest) they send their children to Church of Ireland schools and vote "Protestantly". To them, being Protestant is glamorous, unusual and denotes a certain type of liberal thinking which they find attractive.

Most of my working day is spent writing women's fiction, also described as popular fiction, romantic comedy, commercial fiction, "chick lit", and sometimes rather disparagingly as "airport" or "pulp" fiction. And, like many writers, I write about what I know. My readers comment on the "otherness" of my characters' experiences — the weddings officiated by female clergy, the childhood "dressing-up boxes" (apparently a very Protestant thing!), the phrases and expressions used, the "Protestant" maiden aunts (a very particular kind of gentle yet strong soul) — all which seem perfectly normal to me. And in many ways I suppose my childhood was different to those of my Catholic peers.

There are many other things that make Protestants different and most of these stem back to our early childhoods, and here I am unashamedly talking about cultural observances and not liturgical differences. It is universally accepted (by my friends anyway!) that Protestants do not wash their fruit. This sometimes extends to vegetables, but not always. Whatever the reason, my family has never washed their fruit and neither have most of the Protestant families I know — strange but true. We also sing in church. There's nothing quite like a good Church of Ireland wedding where the whole congregation (except the bemused

Catholics) are singing their little hearts out to "All Things Bright and Beautiful". We eat a lot of plain digestive biscuits apparently, but as I'm not a biscuit fan I couldn't attest to this. And Protestants are excellent timekeepers and are very rarely late for an appointment. It's true!

On a less flippant note, I think that each individual should be allowed to discover religion in his or her own way. The Protestant Church, I feel, allows its members the freedom to do this — to read and interpret the Bible and its stories, to think about and question the meaning of God and His (or Her) place in our lives, to make his or her own decisions on social and moral issues. To me, religion means a lot more than just turning up at church every Sunday. It means being a good Christian and trying to make the world a better place to live in for those close to me, in Ireland and in the rest of the world. It means belonging to a community of Christians — in my own local church and in the wider world context. Religion should be a feeling, a way of thinking, a way of living — no more and no less. As the Dalai Lama once said, "My religion is simple, my religion is kindness".

I have brought up my own son as a free-thinking child in the Church of Ireland tradition. He has been baptised in the local church and, I hope, will choose to be confirmed and will continue to worship in the Church of Ireland tradition when he is older. I have tried to teach him to be a good Christian — as my own parents and grandparents in turn taught me. I am proud of my Protestant background and proud of my different kind of "Irishness".

Michael West

Michael West is a playwright. His work includes Foley, A Play on Two Chairs, The Evidence of Things *and two plays for children:* Forest Man *and* Jack Fell Down. *Among his many adaptations are* Lolita, Death and the Ploughman, The Marriage of Figaro *and* Don Juan. *He is married to Annie Ryan and they have one son.*

Photo by Paul McCarthy

Through A Glass, Darkly

From our family holidays in France I remember vividly the impact of the stained glass windows in Chartres and elsewhere, the cavernous cool gloom of the cathedral illuminated by the brilliant blue and red up above. I was particularly taken with the realisation that the windows were best seen in the dark, away from the light, and that as the day progressed and the balance of darkness tilted to the outside and the gathering night, the windows would drain of colour until one could no longer discern the patterns in the rose, while outside, the vaulted arches now shone with an inner life.

This seems to serve also as an account of memory — the ever-fading glorious image, the shifting perspective, the illuminated partition between light and dark.

I was put in mind of all this the last time I was in St Mary's. My great-uncle Phil led the morning service, strikingly dressed from head to toe in a black cassock, and he preached in a firm, clear voice. My great-uncle has had a long involvement with the Church of Ireland, as he has with most things, since he is a healthy 91 years old.

Later, over Sunday lunch, he spoke of learning to roast a chicken for the first time; of riding an antique bike less than half his age; and wrestling with a cousin of his over 80 years ago — "Boxing" Bob Hilliard — who fell through the skylight and went off to fight Franco.

"Boxing" was one of the kinder epithets bestowed on our illustrious and notorious relation, who became a pastor sometime after his fall and before joining the republicans. He was, according to Phil, always a bit wild, the skylight incident being merely one among many.

What is certainly true is that having given notice of his general temperament, Bob did not let the inconvenience of being an ordained minister interfere with his beliefs.

He caused particular offence in the 1930s when officiating at the marriage of his sister, Mary Hilliard — although I came to know her as Moll Shellard. The offence consisted in Pastor Bob turning up to the reception in the Great Southern in a *suit*, having ditched his ceremonial robes immediately after the service. This deeply disrespectful gesture was compounded by wearing a red tie. Dying in Spain with communists was perhaps a less nuanced challenge to the accepted order, but it seems to have caused no greater surprise than his decision to become a minister in the first place.

Pastor Bob notwithstanding, St Mary's has been fortunate in its faithful servants drawn from my mother's family over the years. It is a fairly modest building, not one renowned for its ornament or beauty, but it is pleasant enough on its corner site on the main street in Killarney. One of my great-uncle Phil's less heralded acts involved commissioning his daughter Frances to touch up the stained glass windows. It had been noted that the eyes of Jesus were fading to white and the Son of God was looking a shade too — for want of a better word — evangelical.

Having an artistic side, Frances was instructed one evening to ink in some gravitas, turning the Lord's eyes back to the world, as it were. While standing on the sill, the church door opened and a woman came in to pray. Of all the pews available to her, she knelt in the one directly beneath the stained glass window with the epileptic Jesus having his sight restored by the frozen artist. Frances could do nothing other than wait for the casual penitent to finish, and so she too stood, head bowed, clasping her hands and her brush, a statue of reverence and respect and patience.

A traveller passing by outside might have looked up at the church that evening and observed the miracle of Jesus opening his eyes; or they might simply have discerned the shadowy figure of an extra disciple in the glass.

The widespread perception of Protestants in southern Ireland has been of just such a figure; a distant, removed, even haughty demeanour behind a partition of privilege and moral certainty. Frequently this perception is held — even cherished — by Protestants themselves, which is more interesting than the more charitable interpretation of these qualities as virtues of decency, uprightness and good manners.

Implicit in all this, however, is the whole notion of the locus of perception: who is doing the looking? And it is this more than the actual opinion held that is important — the sense of the Protestant being the one beheld, the Other, part of a discrete minority, an exception to the rule.

If the human experience is, to use Louis MacNeice's famous phrase, "incorrigibly plural", a single family can contain multitudes. Still, this understanding of the variety of experience is frequently suppressed in favour of tribal alignments, constructs of difference. Such constructs are frequently beautiful, patterned codes that comfort and guide us; they can also be an excuse not to engage with others. For all the restraint and poise and grace I associate with what may be loosely termed "our tradition", I am aware of contrary impulses of withdrawal and the need to be "other".

Some, like Boxing Bob, burst through that partition — whether it is seen as an act of valour or of transgression — and fall to earth among the broken shards; most of us lurk behind it, letting it colour our existence. It is worth remembering, however, that as with stained glass windows, while we need the extremes of night and day to perceive ourselves, the darkness is not always without, nor is there perpetual light within.

Ian White

Ian White was born in Newtownards, County Down, in 1959 and studied youth and community work in the New University of Ulster, Jordanstown. For the last 23 years, he has worked in a range of youth, community and community relations non-governmental organisations in Ireland, both North and south. He is currently very happily living in Dublin with his wife Helen and his four children, Rory, Owen, Jack and Ross.

An Ulster Prod on Irish Sod

I was lucky enough to be born a Presbyterian in Newtownards, County Down. I say "lucky" because to have been a Catholic would have been a very different story as this religious grouping made up only about five per cent of my hometown population. I also was privileged in that I came from a loving family where my mother, who had been adopted at birth, created opportunities through her part-time job as a stitcher for her six surviving offspring which she was never afforded herself. My father was a painter and decorator for 50 years. He died, on retirement, from heart disease which was no doubt caused by the long hours of overtime and nixers, the lead in the paint, the worry of making ends meet and, to a lesser degree, cigarettes.

We were strong churchgoers and I grew up like the rest of the family on a diet of Presbyterian Christianity. The weekly menu included church once or sometimes twice on a Sunday; Sunday School also once or twice; Boys' Brigade on Tuesday nights, Christian Endeavour on Friday night and youth club/fellowship on a Saturday night. On Monday nights, if we were still really hungry, we would supplement our diet with a visit to the James Street gospel hall. Later, as a teenager, whatever free evenings I had were focused mainly on underage drinking and chasing girls.

I remember William Street when the summer was coming. We had two windows on the first floor of our house. As my brothers worked as fitters and welders in Walker's Mill and in the ship-yard, there was no shortage of flag holders to fit to the sills, or flags to put in them. I used my father's ladders to start a window-cleaning round when I was about 15, so I had a kind of love/hate relationship with this particular expression of loyalty. A Union Jack was erected annually and the other flag would change every few years to reflect the changed political, cultural or religious feel-ings and fears. I remember liking the Ulster Vanguard flag. I thought it was more modern looking than the Union Jack. The chimney sweep almost directly across the street always excelled in his demonstration of loyalty. He also had two flags and what seemed like miles of red, white and blue bunting. In some ways, the decoration of the modest houses seemed to make up for the fact that the toilet was at the bottom of the yard and that there was an asbestos roof on the lean-to bathroom.

One summer, when I was about eight years old, I wrote in chalk on the wall of one of the two Catholic families in our street, "Fenians Out". I graduated to the barricades in the Ulster Work-ers' strike some seven years later.

I had left home at 18, so it was easier to escape the rules and conditioning of my community. I met Helen, a Catholic girl from Dublin, and we married in 1981. That year, tensions were high and the tragedy of the hunger strike was happening. I signed the forms issued by the parish priest, which confirmed my support for Helen to raise any children resulting from the marriage as Catholic. We both attended a marriage preparation course organ-ised by St Brigid's Church (this was another precondition that was put on the marriage if it was to happen in the bride's church). I found the course entertaining: where else would you find a mod-ule on family planning delivered by a celibate priest? The course lasted for six weeks, during which time we went to great lengths to keep up the pretence that we were not already cohabiting. I remember the night when a well-selected, well-adjusted middle-class family asked the participants if we had decided whether to attend Mass together as a family or to attend as individuals. I have encountered many such assumptions since moving south.

In 1985, the year our first son was born, we were invited by the UDA to move house from Great Northern Street to a place where mixed marriages would be more acceptable to them. We left the house more or less immediately and shortly after made the decision to move south. The first few years in Dublin were extremely difficult; I was looking for, and sometimes finding (or paranoically believing I had found) evidence of the hostility towards Protestantism and Britishness which I was raised to believe existed in the Republic. There were no symbols that were familiar to me and, worse than this, the most common symbols of national or religious identity used in the south were perceived by my birth community to be aggressive or offensive or both. I have, I believe, adjusted to life in Dublin and cannot envisage living anywhere else, not that I want to. However, this feeling of being "at home" took quite a long time to develop and was not helped by the sectarian republican graffiti which is to be seen throughout Dublin; the national sporting organisation's prohibition of my family becoming members — even though two of my sons are keen players; being told "don't be ridiculous, of course you're not British, you're Irish" (I now have a respect for the British *and* Irish components which make up Ian White); the commonly held perception that all Northern Protestants and unionists were oppressors and privileged (in fact, it was a privilege to grow up in my family and community but I continually feel insulted by the assumption that Protestants *per se* were privileged in socioeconomic terms); the over-simplification of the Troubles and the lack of understanding in the south of the realities of life, not only for Northern unionists but also for Northern nationalists; the sense of "we're all right Jack, sort yourself out 'up there' — we have nothing to do with the problem"; the perceived celebration of martyrdom in Irish history against the celebration of the victories of my tribe.

Some of these irritants have changed, others haven't yet and others perhaps cannot or will not. I enjoy life in the south and now that our roads have improved I can regularly visit all dimensions of my Irishness and Britishness more easily. I am also greatly comforted by the many similarities which exist between both parts of this island. The denial of most people in Northern Ireland to acknowledge the role that they themselves have played in creating or escalating the sectarian conflict is mirrored here in the south. The exclusion of so many people from the institutions of power in the North, and their marginalisation, is alive and well as experienced by Travellers, asylum-seekers, homeless people and many others here in the south. The graffiti that in Northern Ireland tends to insult or threaten people from different religious communities can be compared to the increasing amounts of graffiti here which quite often insults or threatens those from communities which are not Irish, white and Catholic. Exclusive notions of national identity which hold that if you're Irish you can't be British, and vice versa, are thriving all over the island.

It is interesting for me to compare the majority position of the community I was born into with being a member of the minority here in the south. From this experience, I would conclude that the problem surfaces when your identity is perceived to be in jeopardy. It is then that you feel you need it and want to defend and protect it most. Fear of loss of identity is something that the majority must understand in order that all can feel secure and be able to define themselves as they wish. We can all teach our children not just to tolerate or manage diversity, but to welcome it as something that enriches all our lives.

Judith Woodworth

Judith Woodworth was appointed Director of the National Concert Hall in 1993. She first worked in London with a major artist management agency and upon returning to London in the late 1980s she embarked on establishing and promoting the highly successful Celebrity Concert Series at the NCH. She was also Artistic Director of the Music Festival in Great Irish Houses from 1982–99. In 2002, she was appointed a Governor of the Irish Times Trust. She is also a founder member of the Irish branch of the International Women's Forum and a Council member of Alexandra College Dublin.

When I considered the invitation to make a contribution to this publication, my first reaction was: is it not irrelevant nowadays to think about my Protestant background? On greater reflection, my thinking on the subject changed as I cast my mind back to my childhood and teen years in the 1950s and 1960s, when in reality it did feel different to be Protestant.

Both my parents were born before the establishment of the Free State. My mother's family was originally from a rural farming community in County Fermanagh and my father, who was born in 1892, came from a long line of Dublin-based professionals. My father, in particular, saw many dramatic changes take place in Ireland during his long life, and especially a transformation in the dominant role of Protestants in Irish society during the years following 1922. My parents conformed to the custom of the time in sending their three children to Protestant foundation schools. Nevertheless, I am sure that my father would have applauded the dramatic changes of the past 25 years, whereby many Protestant schools, whilst maintaining a traditional liberal Protestant ethos, have become largely interdenominational.

Up to my late teenage years, I had limited opportunities to mix with my Roman Catholic peers. Therefore, my sojourn in the Aran Islands Gaeltacht in 1968 particularly stands out, as we Protestant girls were a small group attending the largely Roman Catholic summer school. Whether we liked it or not, we stood out from the crowd and our difference was remarked on, albeit kindly, by other pupils and our teachers, who in particular had difficulty in comprehending that there were in fact many distinct types of religious belief under the umbrella of Protestantism. (I, in fact, attended a Christian Science church.) However, the heartfelt remarks of our very warm and hospitable *bean an tigh* on our departure caught us completely offside. With tears in her eyes, she explained to us that she was very upset, because lovely girls though we were, we would still all go to Hell eventually, because we were Protestants! We could have received no clearer indication of the status of our minority religion, and even though we greeted her comments with some hilarity at that time, it did give us a moment's pause for reflection that we were really considered outsiders by many of the community.

The 1970s were a time of greater social integration for both my family and myself. With the lifting of the ban on Roman Catholics attending Trinity College, I was able for the first time to meet Catholics on a completely equal footing and from that period developed many lasting relationships. My elder sister Anne's and my own deep involvement in music brought us more into the mainstream of Irish society, since music recognises no religious barriers, except in the strictly liturgical context. During this period, my elder brother Bruce married — a "mixed" marriage and a union which was warmly welcomed by both families. Whilst the arrangements for their marriage were fraught with some difficulties, particularly due to an unhelpful local Roman Catholic cleric, other clerics came together from both religious denominations and performed a beautiful and supportive ceremony.

In the mid-1970s, I emigrated from Ireland to live in London. I recall being somewhat bemused at first that no one had the slightest interest in finding out what religion I was, or that I was a member of the so called "minority" Protestant community. For the first time in my life, I was living in a multi-racial, liberal and mainly tolerant society. I only stood out because I was Irish, not because I was Protestant, and I found this refreshing and liberating.

The Ireland I returned to 12 years later was very different from the one I had left. My Protestant background was largely irrelevant in an increasingly secular and pluralist society. Certainly, I have never felt that my background was any drawback when I applied for the post of Director of the National Concert Hall. Indeed, nowadays legislation ensures there is no discrimination on the basis of gender, race or religion. My Protestantism is now only relevant in the sense that a new generation of Irish people can look at our common Protestant and Roman Catholic heritage and appreciate the beneficial values inherent in both. Nor are Protestants so diffident about being openly proud of being Protestant *as well as* Irish.

I would like to think that the mutual unease of the Protestant and Roman Catholic communities, which was such a feature of my youth, has now largely evaporated — no longer do we feel the need to maintain a barrier on religious grounds. This has been particularly reflected in my own recent experience when my Roman Catholic partner and myself, following our civil marriage, received a blessing of our marriage in the Church of Ireland supported by all our family and friends.

I believe that being a Protestant in the Republic of Ireland is not something to be self-conscious about any longer, except in the sense that being Protestant can contribute in a positive way to the diversity of our society.